THE FIRST
VENTURE
CAPITALIST

THE FIRST VENTURE CAPITALIST

VENTURE

CAPITALIST

Georges Doriot on
Leadership, Capital,
& Business Organization

EDITED BY UDAYAN GUPTA
FOREWORD BY ROBERT MCCABE

GONDOLIER

THE FIRST VENTURE CAPITALIST
© 2004 Udayan Gupta and Bayeux Arts, Inc.
Published by: Gondolier, an imprint of Bayeux Arts, Inc.,
119 Stratton Crescent SW, Calgary,
Canada T3H 1T7 www.bayeux.com

Copy edited by Tim Carroll
Indexed by Moira Calder
Book and jacket design by David Lane

National Library of Canada Cataloguing in Publication
Doriot, Georges F. (Georges Frederic), 1899-1987.

> The first venture capitalist : Georges Doriot on leadership,
> capital, and business organization / Udayan Gupta, editor.

> Includes index.

> ISBN 1-896209-93-9

1. Doriot, Georges F. (Georges Frederic), 1899-1987. 2. Capitalists
and financiers—United States—Biography. 3. Venture capital.
4. Entrepreneurship.

I. Gupta, Udayan, 1950- II. Title.
HG4963.D668 2004   332'.04154'092   C2004-901554-0

First Printing: April 2004
Printed in Canada at Friesens

The ongoing publishing activities of Bayeux Arts, under its "Bayeux" and
"Gondolier" imprints, are supported by the Canada Council for the Arts, the
Alberta Foundation for the Arts, and the Government of Canada through the
Book Publishing Industry Development Program.

The First Venture Capitalist is dedicated to the memory of Georges Doriot who first articulated the role for venture capital in economic development, and to the late Dick Testa who helped keep alive that philosophy.

CONTENTS

FOREWORD

ROBERT MCCABE

HBS Class of '58; partner
Lehman Brothers (1958-1987)

IN DECEMBER 1957, while a student at Harvard Business School, I received a call from Georges Doriot—whom I had never met—inviting me to a Christmas party at his home on Lime Street. A few weeks earlier, I had applied to Lehman Brothers for a job. And now Professor Doriot, whose second-year course at the Business School was known for its intensity and difficulty, was explaining to me that Robert Lehman had just called him to check on me. Since I was *not* taking the course, he thought he would invite me to his house so he could get to know me. All I heard was "NOT TAKING THE COURSE." All I felt was a sense of impending doom.

A few days later, arriving at his unique house on Lime Street—a former blacksmith's shop—I greeted him in French, and much of our conversation for the rest of the evening was in French. If it had not been for my five years of French, I doubt I would have won Professor

Doriot's recommendation for the job. I am sure the direction of my life would have been quite different. My redemption came many years later when Dorothy Rowe, the General's closest confidante at American Research & Development, and I were awarded honorary degrees in the General's "Manufacturing" course at a dinner held at The French Library in Boston.

Over the years, meeting and working with the General and his associates, and many of the General's former students, I did, in fact, develop a sense that I had taken his course. I had the privilege of working very closely with ARD over 30 years, and getting to know the General's philosophy and approach to business intimately. He was an extraordinary individual, with a quiet charisma that made him the trusted adviser of a wide group of businessmen and other leaders. One of his greatest skills was his ability to ask questions that illuminated the critical aspects of an important decision his friends might be facing.

The General was a private person. He deliberately tried to stay out of the limelight. He enjoyed working with his former students, the managements of the companies in which ARD invested, and his friends on a one-to-one basis. He took great pleasure from watching their growing success in business and life. His loyalty to them and his enthusiasm for their work knew no bounds. They were his family. He had no interest in writing books about his management and leadership insights, nor in presenting his memoirs to a wider public.

It is extraordinary that an individual who had such a significant influence over a period of four decades should be so unknown outside the circle of his family of companies and students, and I believe the present work by Udayan Gupta will make a real start in changing that. For those who knew him, it will evoke many memories and will add dimensions to their knowledge of their friend and teacher. For those who did not know him, this material will illuminate an individual who had an enormously productive career as a venture capitalist, teacher, general, and adviser. The inclusion by Mr. Gupta of much previously unpublished source material gives an immediacy and spontaneity to this work that is refreshing. I hope this work will be the first of many that will bring the achievements and teachings of this extraordinary individual to a wide circle.

PREFACE

GEORGES DORIOT WAS NOT the first person to be involved with
venture capital.

In roughly 640 B.C., a pair of Phoenicians decided to settle down in
Miletus (how's that for intergroup mobility!). Their son, Thales,
became a speculator in vegetable oil futures or the rough equivalent
thereof—a form of choice unheard of in pre-urban days. During the
winter when idle oil presses were money-losers for their owners,
Thales "gave deposits for the use of all the olive-presses in Chios and
Miletus, which he hired at a low price because no one bid against him.
When the harvest-time came, and many were wanted all at once and of
a sudden, he let them out at any rate which he pleased, and made a
quantity of money. . . his device for getting wealth is of universal application, and is nothing but the creation of a monopoly." (This description courtesy of a financial reporter named Aristotle.)

More than two thousand years later, King Ferdinand and Queen
Isabella bankrolled a sailor named Christopher Columbus on his
voyages for a piece (a rather substantial piece, some say) of the spoils
his voyages might fetch. The division of the spoils between the general
partner—Columbus—and the limiteds—Ferdinand and Isabella—is
not recorded. But this clearly was ancient venture capital.

Many others including Marco Polo might lay claim to having first thought of the idea of venture capital. But it was Georges Doriot in 1946 who created the first venture-capital institution, regularized the creation of companies, and helped shape it into an organized business strategy. Just as important, he helped train a legion of investors who later established their own venture funds.

Georges Doriot may not have been the first investor of venture capital but he clearly was the first venture capitalist.

In the fall of 2002, when Dick Testa of Testa Hurwitz & Thibeault and the trustee of Georges Doriot's estate asked me to explain the life and work of Professor Doriot, I was intrigued. The task was a challenging one. Not because there was a paucity of material. There was plenty of material. The General was a documentarist, a wonderful letter-writer, and a meticulous keeper of records. He was a biographer's dream.

By any standard, Georges Doriot was a remarkable man. He had many careers, when one of them alone would be enough for most to think they had lived a full life. As a military leader for his adopted United States, he helped to free his native France in World War II. As a Harvard Business School professor, he taught and influenced some of the most important figures of his time, and ours—from Fortune 500 CEOs and successful investment bankers to Wall Street deal makers, politicians, and military strategists.

He was far ahead of his time in understanding business trends and technology change. His investment in Digital Equipment Corporation (DEC) was a daring one, not simply because it was contrarian, but because he saw the investment as a tool for massive economic and technological change.

It wasn't just computer technology that Professor Doriot understood.

He was far ahead of his time in thinking about biology and medicine, recalls venture capitalist Morton Collins who met the General in the 1970s. After Professor Doriot accidentally pricked himself and spilled a drop of blood, he told Collins, "One day everything to know about ourselves will be available in that drop of blood." Medical companies are today proving him so prophetic.

Then there were his five years in charge of the Quartermaster Corps, when he fully transformed its character and its mandate. As with everything else in his life, the men came first.

During the war, Doriot wrote to a Division field observer in a combat zone,

> I have read with very much interest all your letters. I am particularly happy that whenever you have the opportunity, you pay attention to the air forces, the Marines and the Navy. Indeed we must help everyone any time in any way. Be quite certain to tell me anything you might need and keep on advising us as to suggestions we should follow. . . . Do not hesitate to let me know whatever you want that we do not do fast enough or do not do right.

In war or in peace, Georges Doriot proved to be a remarkable manager, organizer and thinker. And his ideas are just as valuable early in this century, as they were in the last.

I wanted *The First Venture Capitalist* to be a sourcebook to Georges Doriot, a book that introduces the reader to his work, to the manner in which others saw him. *The First Venture Capitalist* is an oral history of how Doriot saw the world, of the world he helped to create, and how those all around him saw him. *The First Venture Capitalist* began as the brainchild of Dick Testa who passed away in December 2002. It was Dick who opened the doors and arranged to make the papers and the witnesses available. Elaine Uzan Leary of The French Library helped to administer the grant from the Beaucourt Foundation, while Testa Hurwitz's Bill Asher and Peter Wilson provided both support and readings. Students of General Doriot, entrepreneurs who were part of ARD's investment portfolio, venture capitalists who had worked with

General Doriot at ARD and many others helped in piecing together this ambitious effort. Ken Olsen and Aulikki Olsen gave their time, their thoughts and a long-forgotten interview.

The First Venture Capitalist would also not have been possible without the help of Claude Janssen and Arnaud de Vitry who gave generously of their time and their memories. As we came close to the end, David Lane not only helped to design the book, but also gave it its unique shape and character, and Tim Carroll, a former colleague at *The Wall Street Journal,* pitched in to help edit the text.

The completion of the book, especially after the untimely death of Dick Testa, is greatly due to Bob McCabe, whose personal and business relationship with Doriot extended over decades. McCabe, who as a partner at Lehman Brothers, worked on many ARD deals, opened new doors and provided both insight and encouragement. The book also could not have happened without the help of Bayeux Arts, Ashis and Swapna Gupta and most of all, my wife, Kathy.

PROLOGUE

ASK ANY MAJOR PUBLISHER what it takes to bring out a book about a person like General Georges F. Doriot, and you'll probably receive a response that goes like this: "General who? Ah! It's true that Georges Doriot was a remarkable and prescient man. Unfortunately, though, it's our feeling here that, as influential and important as he was, he just isn't a big-enough 'name' for a book about him to get the critical and commercial attention it would need for us to launch it successfully."

In the context of contemporary media's fascination with Andy Warhol's "In the future everybody will be famous for 15 minutes," it is easy to present fleeting figures—famous and infamous—as publishing fodder. But it is both ignorant and foolhardy not to recognize the profound importance of Doriot in the financing and shaping of America's entrepreneurial economy and in the creation of a culture for corporate America.

"His influence has stayed with me forever," says William Lucas, the former CEO of Carnation. Lucas echoes the feelings of hundreds of Harvard Business School graduates who took Doriot's "Manufacturing," never fully recognizing that the man who insisted they show up on time and properly dressed was infusing them with a philosophy of business that went beyond mastering accounting rules, marketing principles and finance. The lectures the Professor gave and the lessons he provided are exemplary in that they represent a world of business deeply rooted in strong moral principles and social responsibility.

Those who can, do, those who can't, teach, the saying goes. In the world of business, they take the saying one step further: Those who can't, become consultants. In this world, Doriot was unusual. He was one of "those who can" who actually did. In a world in which the financing of risk and innovation was random and haphazard at best, Professor Doriot brought clarity and introduced a system into the financing of risk and innovation.

He recognized several key elements in the process. Real companies take time to build. Young companies need several rounds of equity—not debt. Most importantly, treat shareholders—the ones who take the risk to provide equity capital—right.

"He did everything he could to make sure shareholders got treated properly," says Bob McCabe, whose personal and business relationship with Doriot extended over decades. Everything meant keeping costs and salaries down. ARD professionals worked long and hard for salaries and rewards that are a pittance compared with the ones regularly awarded to those in the venture-capital business today. He realized that if shareholders didn't get rewarded for the risks they took—before everyone else—there just wouldn't be a future. "There was an integrity to him that was unique," says McCabe.

In a world in which the social role of business has been overwhelmed by the demands of profit and a quick buck, Professor Doriot's message is even more prescient. Entrepreneurship, risk capital and economic well-being are interconnected, he contended. Opportunistic entrepreneurship that puts profit before the building of value and shareholder interests cannot be sustained. Similarly, shareholder greed that shortchanges a company's well-being can create short-term profits at best, but no long-term profitability.

There are those who dismiss Doriot's achievements as a venture capitalist. He was a "one-trick pony," referring to his massively successful investment in Digital Equipment Corporation But Professor Doriot had more tricks than DEC in his bag. ARD and its affiliates, European Enterprises Development Company (EED) and Canadian Enterprise Development Corporation Limited (CED) were looking at a wide array of technology investments—many far ahead of their time. And DEC itself, with Ken Olsen as its chief executive and Professor Doriot's ARD as its largest shareholder, was a pioneering innovator in technology and the management of technology.

Allan Conway, Harvard Business School alumnus and professor of strategy at the Haskayne School of Business in Calgary, says that Professor Doriot looked at business leadership as an interactive mix of mind (analysis), heart (personal attraction and commitment), and soul (values and ethics). He approached business on a variety of fronts—business as a process of analysis, business as personal leadership, and the importance of ethics and social responsibility to business success.

Professor Doriot believed in investing for the long term, notes Conway. "The noble task is to build constructively in the hope that capital gains will be the reward for intelligent, hard work." Cultures and economies "cannot live off the enterprise and vision of preceding generations only." For Doriot, venture capital and new venture development were first and foremost a strategic investment.

Contemporary histories of venture capital credit the likes of Laurence Rockefeller and Jock Whitney for giving shape to the venture-capital process. But well before Rockefeller and Whitney, Professor Doriot, a French-born Harvard Business School professor, and Ralph Flanders, a New England industrialist turned banker and politician, had thought of the idea of a pool of capital to be invested in emerging companies that were still in their infancy. World War II stalled their plan but, immediately after the war, the pair launched their venture-capital fund, American Research & Development.

The fund that Doriot and Flanders designed was no arcane financial instrument. It was an attempt to design a tool that would finance business development, especially in the uncharted waters of high technology—without government involvement. ARD was also designed to allow public participation. At the time, no such investment vehicle existed, certainly none that was publicly traded, yet Doriot managed to create one. And he persuaded some of the most prestigious financial and industrial institutions of the day to join as investors.

The fund's first board of advisers consisted of three scientific pioneers, all from the Massachusetts Institute of Technology. They were Karl T. Compton, then president of MIT; Jerome Hunsaker, who taught the first course in aeronautical engineering and aviation design at MIT, and in 1914 developed the first modern wind tunnel in the United States; and Edwin Gilliland, renowned for his work in electro-chemistry, ion exchange and electrodialysis. Gilliland later became president of Ionics, one of ARD's portfolio companies.

The roster of investors was just as impressive. It included insurers John Hancock Mutual Life Insurance Company, Home Insurance Company, and State Mutual Life Assurance Company; industrial corporations Crane Company, Hormel Inc., Godfrey L. Cabot, and West Virginia Paper & Pulp Company; and educational institutions like MIT, University of Pennsylvania, University of Rochester and Rice Institute. Also among the investors were Commonwealth International Corporation, Consolidated Investment Trust, Graham-Newman Corporation, Investors Mutual, Massachusetts Investors Trust and Massachusetts Investors Second Fund. Some of these companies no longer exist, but their work lives on.

The rationale for this corporate and institutional involvement was an investment in economic development and future prosperity. Wrote Ralph Flanders:

> The postwar prosperity of America depends in a large measure on finding financial support for that comparatively small percentage of new ideas and developments which give promise of expanded production and development and an increased standard of living for the American people. We cannot float along indefinitely on the enterprise and vision of preceding generations.

Doriot and Flanders may have benefited from the renewed energy and spirit in the aftermath of a victorious war, but they also presented a real vision and purpose for venture capital. They didn't promise easy money, but the rewards for being early investors and initial risk takers could assuredly be enormous. The most significant part of the "sell" was that Professor Doriot convinced major industrial corporations to consider venture capital as a strategic investment, not merely an alternative asset class that deserved a nominal allocation.

Professor Doriot may have been among the first to recognize the strategic role of the entrepreneurial business in the economy, and the synergies possible between the big corporation and more modest entrepreneurial endeavors. In his "Manufacturing" course at the Harvard Business School he regularly discussed how the two—big corporations and entrepreneurial endeavors—interacted with one another.

Many entrepreneurs were born, or reborn, after having been stifled working for large corporations. They were men with ideas and ambition that large corporations simply didn't know how to accommodate. Why would a skilled and ambitious manager want to work at a corporate job to which the corporation itself didn't accord visible value? The professor was among the first to recognize the spiritual needs that entrepreneurship fulfilled and the tools technology provided to fulfill those needs.

He also recognized the nature of the corporate role. Without the corporation as a customer and a user of their products, most small businesses couldn't grow. Equally important, the first adoption of most new technology was at an institutional level, and most likely within a large corporation.

Professor Doriot had also been a part something even bigger than the biggest corporations: the United States government. During World War II, in his role now as the General, Doriot had helped to resupply the people who resupply the armed forces—the Quartermaster Corps. But, back when he returned to being the Professor, Doriot wasn't sure that government organizations were appropriate customers for young businesses. He found government, even the Army, too complacent in its decision-making. Time and again he referred to the government sector as anti-development and warned that investment excesses could lead to government intervention and even greater inefficiencies.

Doriot did not have faith in government and regulation. Years later, his battles with the Securities and Exchange Commission would leave him frustrated and angry. Still, his experiences in the Army played a major role in shaping his attitude toward business and business management.

The War started in Europe on September 1, 1939. In 1940, Doriot became a naturalized U.S. citizen and began helping the United States War Department create the Army Industrial College. A year later, one of his Harvard Business School students, the Quartermaster General, Major General Edmund B. Gregory, helped him obtain a direct appointment as Lieutenant Colonel. Doriot began work as Chief of the Military Planning Division, Office of the Quartermaster General.

Doriot brought tremendous dynamism and imagination to his task in the Quartermaster General's office. He relished the role of a planner. When fighting began in Europe he had visited the French Embassy in Washington to volunteer to fight. But a desk officer informed him that at age 40 he was too old to be a combatant and instead offered him a job as a chauffeur, if he so desired. Doriot went back to Boston, became a naturalized United States citizen and shortly afterward ended up in the Quartermaster General's office, where his spirit of scientific inquiry and keen insight won him immediate respect.

Doriot studied the state of U.S. Army equipment and found it unready and inappropriate for the war that was being fought. In 1941, at a symposium Doriot said "Many items, which had been developed as the result of field experience in the mud and rain of Northern France in 1917 and 1918 were modified in peacetime to be more suitable for the garrison life at Fort Benning, Georgia, or Fort Sam Houston, Texas." He complained that those in charge, even after the outbreak of war in Europe did not recognize the importance of immediately improving existing equipment.

It wasn't *carte blanche* for the native Frenchman. But he found a way out. He recruited for his division by going through the lists of those who had attended Harvard Business School. He then brought together leaders in mountaineering and arctic expedition and leaders of business research and industry. And to everyone he posed the question "what if . . ." in order to imagine every possibility that U.S. soldiers could confront in widespread combat.

It wasn't enough just to come up with new equipment. The Army required that all item requests be accompanied by a list of approved people to produce it, a statement of funds availability, and approval from the overtaxed War Production Board. Once again, Doriot used his network to make sure that companies offered their expertise and facilities. He also found university laboratories willing to contribute their research to the development programs. A process that had stalled, and had no champions to help restart it, suddenly took off under the leadership of Doriot.

The Division's accomplishments under General Doriot included the development of all new uniforms and equipment for use in every kind of climate and geographic region around the world; a whole family of new field rations (for example, B-, C-, D-, and K-Rations, 5-in-1s, 10-in-1s, Assault and Accessory Packs) along with stoves, food containers, openers, and cook tents for various climates. These planners also pioneered in the development of new plastic items, water-resistant and flameproof fabrics, and many synthetic goods for use in place of precious natural resources.

Quartermaster Hall of Fame citation

The war experience was an important one for Doriot. His role in the Quartermaster General's office and his subsequent promotion to Brigadier General helped him within the HBS sphere as well. "We were impressed and in awe," recalls John Whitehead, who was a student of his in 1948. "It was after the war and there were a lot of veterans in the class but none of them was a general."

More important than the title of general was the organizational knowledge and experience from World War II that Doriot brought into his teaching and his work. Whitehead remembers his very organized, almost martial approach to teaching "Manufacturing," the best-attended course at HBS.

Doriot would stand behind curtains until the entire class was seated. Then the doors would be closed, the lights dimmed and the General would make his entrance. Says Whitehead, "It never failed to make an impact."

In later years, as Doriot pursued his dream of a global business school, he would tout the Harvard case method as the way to go. But Doriot himself was one HBS professor who never used the case method.

Instead, his class was a mix of practical tips, advice, people, and issues. Doriot wanted his students to realize that they would play an important role—the very nature of HBS mandated it—but he also wanted them to recognize a larger role for themselves, a role he continually seemed to fulfill for himself.

Years later, on the eve of his departure from HBS he would reflect on his role as a teacher:

"Thinking again of the Manufacturing course, I really have no
anything. All I have done is to realize that the young men who were kind
enough to take a course with me were rather remarkable and very prom-
ising. They were willing to work and were above average in human characteristics and general ability. They also seem to have a rather practical
sense. Therefore, I believed that what I should do was to give them an
opportunity to develop and show to themselves, to businessmen, and to
me that they could do above average work both in quantity and quality.
Sometimes I had to drive them, but they always responded. I am
extremely proud of them, and I believe that they were, generally speaking, the best men in the School. That was not due to me—it was due to
them. All I did was to try to provide the environment—the desire-the
willpower and the pride in superior work.

Often later on, after they had left me, in some cases I wondered
whether they had not reached a maximum while in the School. Perhaps,
business was not using them as they could be used—perhaps the environment, the drive and push, were not there anymore. I know what those
men could do because they had done it and done it in a practical way
with the company studies and the topic report. I know they wanted to be
challenged and that if they were, they would do so much, so well, so
constructively.

The missionary in Doriot always believed that business wasn't simply
dollars and cents, it was about building now and for the future.

Let us do more than our share for the generations following us.
Do we want to build or merely enjoy what others ahead of us have
made possible? Really, how can one enjoy anything if one is not
building for the future of others? Remember that our happiness is in
direct proportion to the contributions we make. Do not forget those
who have not had the educational advantage you have had. Teach
whenever you can in high school, in college. Help high school graduates with the same kind of help and advice you received at the
Business School.

Help building fine citizens and be one of them. I hope for many years
to be building with you. May I end with one of the stories I have used in
class with you.

On a road somewhere—three men were breaking stones. They were asked what they were doing.
One said, "I earn my living."
One said, "I break stones."
One said, "I help build cathedrals."
Let us build cathedrals together.

Not only was Doriot building cathedrals, but he was also training their architects. From 1928 to 1966, Doriot helped educate some of America's most successful captains of industry. Philip Caldwell, former chairman of Ford Motor Company, once noted.

He taught me how to think. More importantly, he taught me to think. The things he taught me are more important thirty-five years out of school than they were when I began my career. By any measure, you'd have to say that General Doriot was one of the greatest of teachers.

Doriot didn't believe in much leisure and his own work style and teachings conveyed that. In describing to his students the working habits of Harley Curtis, a president of General Motors, Doriot said:

While he was president of GM, Mr. Curtis spent only weekends with his family. Mondays he commuted to Detroit in one of eighteen planes at his disposal and worked steadily from 8 a.m. to 7 p.m. and did not return to his home until Friday evening. That's anti-modern, isn't it? Your hopes and expectations are [to work] from 9 to 4:30 and at 4:40 you'll be getting ready, and you only want those working hours from Tuesday to Friday night—or Friday noon. Friday afternoon you want to think about the weekend, and Monday you're too tired to work anyway. So, that's that. I know your reaction. Your reaction is, well, he didn't give enough to his family, and I suppose some of you will say, he died at 59 years of age of a heart attack. I have never seen, with all the friends I have had, any connection between hard work and heart attacks. As a matter of fact, the last two men I know who died from heart attacks died after their retirement, I think from the shock of having nothing to do.

Doriot's workweek stretched across seven days, instead of the customary five. "We should give beauty to the word "work," he would say. "Leisure is a fake." And he expected his fellow workers and employees to follow suit. Venture capitalist Dan Holland remembers Doriot expecting all of the ARD personnel to routinely show up on Saturdays. "I don't think he thought we had families or children," he recalls.

Ironically, Doriot was an avowed family man. Not only was he devoted to his wife Edna—he published a set of his love poems to her— he counseled all of his students to make sure that they and their families were in sync. During the war he also took care of Anne and Alice, two children by French Prime Minister Paul Reynaud. Reynaud asked Doriot to care for them because he was afraid for their safety in France.

Without families working together, no corporate mission would be successful, Doriot believed. "I wish you would invite your wives to class because it will give them a chance to find out what your work is all about and it might help you team up in life. You can also bring a girl, if you are really interested in her because it might help you reach a decision."

In spite of the fact that Doriot directed his remarks at men—a practice typical of the time—Doriot was well ahead of his time in the value he placed in women. Dorothy Rowe, his administrative assistant at ARD, was one of his closest confidantes and became treasurer of Digital Equipment Corporation after ARD's investment in the company. Rowe, with the support of Doriot, was the highest-ranking female executive in a technology business in her time.

Doriot recognized the role that technology could play, not simply in the creation of wealth for investors, but in the entire development process. And more than anyone of his time, he understood the implications of building real businesses out of technology and the economic transformation that it could bring about.

The General's investments in technology were not long shots he hoped would pay off, they were often the results of months of painstaking research. Doriot's projects—for his students as well as the ARD staff—often consisted of students researching areas that Doriot felt would become significant in the future.

He thrived on the new and the untested. And he would often go out on a limb to invest in new ideas, fully cognizant that his own board might be hard-pressed to recommend the investment.

That certainly was the case with ARD's historic $70,000 investment Digital Equipment Corporation in 1957. Doriot presented the investment as one that would make existing computers more efficient, not one that could create a new generation of computers. Doriot had tremendous confidence in Ken Olsen, the founder and the scientific spirit behind DEC and gave him all the support he could. Still, no one could have imagined the significance of DEC and its line of computers. Certainly no one could have imagined how that $70,000 would change the face of computing.

As far back as the 1950s, Doriot also experimented in global venturing, forming venture-capital funds in Canada and in Europe. Canadian Enterprise Development Corporation Limited (CED) was formed in the autumn of 1962 with an initial capital investment of $5 million. European Enterprises Development Company (EED) was formed in December 1963 "in the belief that there is a need in Europe for a source of long-term venture capital for new and existing businesses, particularly when they are to exploit new technological, merchandising, or service ideas."

EED was modeled after ARD. In explaining its *raison d'etre*, Doriot wrote,

> The growth of a company, a country, or indeed a community depends on the vision and enterprise of its people. At this stage in the development of European nations, it is all-important to encourage imaginative and progressive men with ideas and with fresh concepts, to create successful new enterprises. This will not only expand production and employment, but also give such men the opportunity to build new com-

panies and develop existing ones. Every day ideas are being developed with industrial and commercial potentialities. It is important that those with promise of success are teamed up with individuals who have the ability to help them germinate, grow and develop into profitable business organizations.

Neither Europe nor Canada was ready for venture capital. The financial institutions didn't seem to have the flexibility or the risk profile necessary for long-term investing in emerging companies, especially in technology. Indeed, when small companies ran into problems, as many invariably did, the solutions offered were too conventional and cookie cutter to be helpful. "The approach was too banking-oriented and not enough venture capital," recalls Arnaud de Vitry, one of Doriot's students who was on the board of directors of EED.

In truth, both the European and the Canadian efforts were about Doriot the globalist, a transplanted Frenchman in America who saw his world in global terms. Doriot often told his students:

> Just realize that I am doing it [teaching] because I think that people, knowing I came to America from France—nobody asked me to come— were nice to me and I stayed here. Therefore, as long as I can do something which is useful to others, I would like to do it.

It was the spirit of globalism that also got Doriot and his wife involved in the metamorphosis and expansion of The French Library in Boston. The Library had been organized in 1940 after the war began in Europe to promote cultural relations between the United States and France. In 1961, it was moved to 53 Marlborough Street, a 1860s mansion donated by a wealthy benefactor. Then Edna Doriot became involved, became president, and, with her husband's support, completely transformed the scope and mission of the Library. It was Edna's enthusiasm and energy that helped the library acquire the adjacent building and join it to create the current Library complex. When Edna died in 1978, Professor Doriot took over the role of president and brought to it the same spirit of dynamism and organization with which he infused his other tasks. Indeed, until the Doriot papers were donated to MIT in the fall of 2003, they became part of The French Library's collection, adjacent to the works of filmmaker Marcel Carne, best known for his *Les Enfants du Paradis*.

This vision of bridging cultures was also the heart of INSEAD, the business school that Doriot helped launch in Fontainebleau in 1959.

Europe never had a tradition of postgraduate business education. And although there were very large industrial organizations on the Continent, the idea that managers could be trained in a pedagogical setting—in parallel with learning on the job—was a novel one. Still, as early as 1926, Doriot had begun thinking about the need to teach business management in Europe. At first, he merely wanted to introduce the program in an existing school, but he found no takers among existing institutions. One French professor who visited the Harvard Business School went back totally unimpressed. "He went right back to Paris telling me that Descartes had figured it out several years back," Doriot later recalled.

The solution came from the Paris Chamber of Commerce. After several years of back and forth, the Chamber decided that it would help establish a school that would be similar to HBS in its structure and purpose. While the idea of a business school was new for the Chamber, founding schools wasn't, notes Jean-Louis Barsoux in his "INSEAD: From Intuition to Institution." The Chamber "had a dynamic tradition of founding schools, counting among its successes both the *Ecole des Hautes Etudes Commerciales* and the *Ecole Superieure de Commerce de Paris*," says Barsoux.

Doriot spent the summer of 1929 working with Pierre Jolly of the Chamber of Commerce translating Harvard cases to be used at the new school. The following year, Doriot sent the curriculum to Harvard for approval. In response, Harvard sent Edna Allen, a young research assistant to help organize the material and prepare the school for opening. Doriot returned to the U.S. and at the end of that year married Edna. The new business school known as the *Centre de Perfectionnement aux Affaires* (CPA) opened in October 1930.

CPA was possibly the first business school designed for middle-management executives and by all accounts it was a monumental success. But it would take another 25 years before the CPA would evolve into a full-fledged business school. Today, INSEAD is one of Europe's most-respected business schools and holds its own among the world's best.

THE TEACHER

H ARVARD BUSINESS SCHOOL has had many celebrated professors, captivating orators, brilliant thinkers, extraordinary commentators but few have compared with Georges Doriot.

Doriot was the consummate teacher, one who taught a unified philosophy of management, not a specialized course in accounting or finance or production or marketing. He talked about business practices, global competition, ethics, and family—an odd mix of issues. He was convinced that if students were to succeed in business they had to see their work as part of a larger mission. Businesses exist because they serve a larger purpose, not simply to make money. And those who failed to remember that would, in the long run, hurt themselves and the environment they operated in.

At a time when business schools admitted mostly men, Doriot addressed the career concerns of his male students but also recognized their need to approach careers with respect to their families. His legendary lectures to spouses were pioneering attempts to place family and career goals in a harmonious context. "It got to the point that the year after I graduated he held five evening sessions for the wives of the students to tell them what was required of the businessman," recalls Jordan Golding, HBS class of '50, who later became a partner with Peat Marwick.

During his tenure at the Harvard Business School, Doriot taught students who later became some of the most influential men in corporate America. And even those who were at Harvard and didn't take his Manufacturing course didn't fail to be touched. "There was something magical about him," recalls Bob McCabe, an HBS student who didn't take the course. McCabe, who later became the banker to many of the deals that Doriot put together, remembers Doriot as the one HBS professor who dared to talk about the reality of business and business life. "He taught what he knew and what he knew was remarkable," says McCabe. Years later, Doriot awarded an "honorary degree" to McCabe and his longtime assistant Dorothy Rowe.

"He was a bigger-than-life figure," says John Whitehead, later a co-chair and senior partner of Goldman Sachs and now the head of the Lower Manhattan Development Corporation. "He was the biggest name on the faculty and every second-year student should take his course. I succumbed to those blandishments," says Whitehead, HBS Class of '47.

And Felipe Propper, HBS Class of '53, another student who later went to work on Wall Street, remembers Doriot teaching globalism. "His examples were from all over. He taught us the need for an organization that could react to changes, not only in the U.S., but the world over. He understood the need for a global organization much earlier than most of his contemporaries did," says Propper.

At a time when teaching business disciplines was still in its infancy, Doriot had a head start over his contemporaries. He was a French-born, naturalized American who spoke more than one language, he grew up inside one of the 20th century's most significant industries—his father was an engineer at auto maker Peugeot; he was an organization man who had helped to redesign the Army's Quartermaster Corps during World War II; and he was a developmentalist who helped start one of the first institutional venture-capital funds, Doriot wasn't teaching theory, "he was teaching practice," says Propper.

"You took Manufacturing not for Manufacturing, but for Doriot," says Jordan Golding, who remembers Doriot as one of the most-influential persons in his life. Recalls Golding:

> At that point in time all the courses used the case study, except for General Doriot's. It was basically a lecture course. It gave him a chance to talk about his own philosophy of management. It was a very compelling course, different from all that the others had to offer.
>
> Doriot didn't tolerate any stragglers or auditors. He would come in and look around the classroom and would kick out those who were simply visiting. Either you took his course or didn't.
>
> He challenged you mentally, making you think about business in the context of everything else that was going on. At the time the Chinese communists were overrunning China. Chiang Kai-Shek was still there. The General gave us an assignment asking what the Chinese could do— short of war—to stop the challenge of the Red Chinese.

THE MANUFACTURING LECTURES

To Doriot, Manufacturing wasn't simply factories and machines and lathes, it was the heart of business. It's how you created value and development and wealth. Sixty years ago, in a classroom at the Harvard Business School, this is what he said to his students as he began the course:

In this class, I hope I will be able to teach you and help develop an attitude that will be useful in Manufacturing. I want you to have an ability to pick and lead people in such a way that they will do things they did not think they could do. This is the quality of a great business leader.

To help you develop this attitude I would like to emphasize several important factors. First, you must train yourselves to be imaginative. You must look beyond to see objects which you can improve. To do this, you have to realize the needs for which the object is made. In other words, you have to determine the functional requirements of the object—learn to think about how it was made, why it was made, who is going to use it, and how it is going to be used. Then on the basis of these functional requirements try to see how you could make the object better in a different form and different material. Be critical of what you see but do not stop at criticism. Attempt to improve.

Next, you must be able to get correct information. I do not expect you to know many specific facts but I will insist that you know where to find them. Furthermore you must have enough general information to stay abreast of new business developments. You must have this technique of staying informed in order to be a manufacturer. In order to develop it you have to start now determining methods of finding out what is going on in the world and who is getting things done in the world.

You have to find out who you can rely upon for correct facts. And when you need to know something next year it may be too late to get the background information you need. A man trying to catch a streetcar must run alongside of it so that he will be able to jump on unhurt. If he tried to stand and grab it as it went by, then he might break an arm or leg. So it is in business. If you have been aware of the world around you, then you will be able to meet new problems as they come along.

Finally, you must be able to prepare yourselves for crisis. The shoeshine operator in Harvard Square can operate his business without taking into account a multitude of factors that might lead to disaster. He has a simple business with few problems. Raw materials and advertising do not worry him much. But for all the rest of us in business we must expect a continuation of crises. You cannot face these successfully until you have the imagination and the right information beforehand to prepare yourself. However, on the threshold of the crisis it takes courage, stamina and fortitude in order to be successful. You young men must decide now whether or not you have these qualities essential to the make-up of a good manufacturer.

It takes a strong physical man and a tough-minded individual to produce goods, but if you have these qualities and the determination to do well, if you will not be soft in the face of trial, if you will never be half-hearted and will never shirk your duty, then you will have the privilege of the greatest profession I know: converting plain material into useful, beautiful, helpful products.

This takes some of the greatest qualities man possesses, but it also pays high returns in creative satisfaction.

THE BUSINESS FRAMEWORK

If the art of warfare demands, among other things, a readiness for confronting the unexpected, Georges Doriot's understanding of the complexities of contemporary business was also founded on a willingness to take on challenges of every kind. In Doriot's business philosophy, an appetite for change and progressive innovation was more important than a quest for stability and security. He treated problems as opportunities for transformational change.

Doriot's ideas on such topics as "a concept of business," "an international frame of reference," a "national frame of

reference," and "the technological framework" were truly
pioneering. Judged in the context of today's management
beliefs and practices, Doriot's thoughts might well be consid-
ered iconoclastic by some observers.

The Concept of Business

Today I would like to give you my concept of business. Many people
have published articles about the establishment of business as a science.
I think this is misleading. I would rather look at business as an art in
which science is becoming more and more useful. Of course, we do
have specialized subjects such as accounting and statistics, which lend
themselves to scientific techniques. However, business management on
a whole cannot yet be classified as a science.

Suppose we asked four artists to paint the same landscape. Probably
each one would have his own ideas on mixing paints and the kind of
materials to use and each would no doubt have his way of interpreting
what he saw. Looking at the finished paintings we might see all sorts of
variations from severe modern work to an 18th-century style. Yet in
judging the four pictures we might consider each one very good.

As there is no definite criteria by which we can appraise these paintings, so I believe there are no sets of rules by which we can judge the
operation of business. Businesses may be run differently and still be
equally well-run. The search for standardization leads to a quest for
security. This quest makes you a worthless businessman. Furthermore,
I want you young men to realize that you are more important to business than you would be if you would merely follow rules for good management. Because each problem requires new thinking for its solution,
you must be a much better man to manage a business than if you could
only follow simple instructions.

You know, every eight years or so we get an idea which we think will change everything in the art of management. First we had the Taylor system to cure all business ills. Every school in the country taught the Taylor system. While Taylor himself had some very good suggestions his followers got so fanatical that they thought they could tackle any business problem by this one device.

Frederick Taylor's scientific management techniques were designed to break down complicated tasks into a series of simple tasks that could be systematized to take advantage of the cheap labor from an uneducated work force. Once the tasks were divided and specified, each task could be taught to a worker who could perform it by rote, and the application of analytic techniques, such as time studies, could further optimize the task performance.

But soon we found that the Taylor system was not infallible. An early hint of this came from Providence, Rhode Island, where a business adopted the Taylor system. After a week they had to close the plant. Upon closer inspection they found that a girl in the office, who had to sort cards by color, was color blind and causing all of the confusion.

So, after the Taylor system, we settled down for a short time until the statisticians took over. We thought then that our troubles had become insurmountable because we did not have enough information. So businessmen hired statisticians, who sent out questionnaires, stopped people on the street, counted noses, and printed big thick volumes of figures. Within a short time we knew how many people brushed their teeth between 8:00 and 8:15 in the morning and how many women with red hair crossed the corner of 42nd and Broadway on Mondays from 10:00 to 10:15. But still businesses flopped and the statisticians could not always tell us why.

The next answer to the business dilemma came from the economists. Now businessmen began hiring these people by the score, and these new saviors in turn filled the walls of our offices with every

conceivable kind of curve. No business could operate without subscribing to the best economics journals. But still businesses went bust. The
fact that the year was 1929 helped to speed up this process. Very shortly
business saw that the economists did not have the only answers.

But now we find that all business problems are really human problems. Now we are being told that if we solve the human difficulties our
business worries are over. I hope to show you later on that this thinking is as dangerous as that kind which in turn accepted the Taylor
system, the statistician and the economist as the absolute remedy for all
difficulties. Of course, a worker will not be able to perform well if he is
put in a room where the fumes are so bad that he cannot breathe, and
naturally his morale will drop if he works on a machine where he is
liable to be hurt. But I believe that many of these human problems
come about as a result of technical errors.

Now, do not think that I consider each of these remedies as foolish
and unimportant. Each one is very important in the proper dosage,
although none is the complete answer to business difficulty and none
can remove the cause of business failure.

Try to get the idea that fixed assets are really liabilities. When you
think of a manufacturing company you probably see it as a big plant
with many buildings. It looks like a very stable, permanent thing. Yet
that concept is very dangerous because in truth the manufacturing
company is not fixed at all. The most impressive manufacturing business I ever saw was one in Cleveland where a man manufactured pills.
He had one supplier make the pills, he hired an advertising agency to
take care of the promotion, and he handled the administration with a
very small office force. He had a perfect set-up, one where he could be
flexible enough to avert most causes for failure.

A business is really an amalgamation of all sorts of assets. Men are
about your best assets. Research and design can be great advantages,
and your company's ability to sell may be a great asset. Yet the accountant's balance sheet does not show these qualities as assets. Later I will

try to show you that a bank loan can be a great asset to a company because it represents a very valuable connection with one of your best friends, the banker. Yet the accountant calls it a liability. So forget these rigid concepts which you have learned and try to see business in a different light.

My idea of a business is that it floats like a balloon in instable equilibrium pushed about by awfully nasty things. These things, gentlemen, are raw materials, new processes, technical evolution, public demand, government regulations and restrictions, politics, and all types of events on an international scale. We cannot measure or forecast these many forces. Furthermore, their relative strength varies sharply from one time to another. Try to imagine the picture of this balloon being pushed and tossed about by these many pressures constantly changing.

So what is our job? First, we have to know what these forces are and we must try to dodge them and diminish their strength. We must be able to turn these forces around so that they act in our best interests rather than against our best interests. Somehow we have to cut down part of their strength.

Secondly, we must determine a goal. This goal cannot be a fixed target but must appear as a zone. It is not a star in the sky but rather it is the direction in the sky towards which we must move. After we have set up this goal then we must create boundaries. Though our pattern toward the goal is a wavy line we cannot go beyond these boundaries. Sometimes a situation will come up forcing us outside of our boundaries. When this happens we must have our eyes open and realize that if we go outside of the original boundaries we must then set up a new goal. Suppose we were making shoes in the $18-$24 range. If we find that we cannot compete well in this market, we might start making shoes in the $10 class. However, when we do this we must realize that we are outside of our boundary and that we must work toward this new goal of producing shoes for a different market.

Thirdly, we must drive towards our goal. This effort is really the art of spending money so that we give each dollar a meaning. To do this we must be cost-conscious—find out what things should cost. Do not think of cost in terms of dollars; rather consider it in terms of effort or value.

Finally, we must find out what possibilities we have to reach the goal. We want to find out what risks are involved in our effort towards it. We have to determine ways of checking our progress along the path. I do not want to give you the idea that we can weigh all the risks involved and then flip a coin to determine what we must do. You cannot arrive at decisions that easily. After weighing all of these risks you still must determine the best course of action and then pursue it with courage and great determination.

Do you know what the worst thing is in manufacturing? It is the uncertainty. With this concept I find that I am able to check the danger of uncertainty by knowing some of the forces which make it disastrous. Remember the story of the four artists. Business is an art because nothing is ever certain, but for that reason it makes you much more important.

Success does not always come to a man because he is wise. If you look around you can find many people who have been successful in business who are not necessarily the most intelligent men you meet. I am not sure why this is true, but it is a fact that some people are very lucky. Some men seem to generate good luck. I think that this results because they have an ability to be so keen that they can see an opportunity and then grab it. The superior man, the winner, is the man who saw an opportunity when other people did not and then he did something about it. Lesser men, looking at his success, might call it good luck.

Effort takes much drive and push. It takes a tremendous desire to grow, to do things differently. You must feel this drive within you and try to develop an interest in those things that will give you the push you need for success. However, nothing is more tiring than a professional driver. The best driver is the one who is so relaxed that the people around him are not conscious of his drive. This drive must be genuine; it must help other people to do better.

These outside forces that make up the framework are worth studying because they form an atmosphere in which you must work. You must learn about these outside forces. You must determine what particular kind of framework you will fit into and what problems you will likely face. I admit that it is very hard to know what these problems might be.

Your difficulty will not be in solving problems. It will be in knowing which problems are most difficult and oftentimes in knowing where the most important problems are. Many able people can solve every problem that comes to them. They fail because they do not develop means of detecting the presence of hidden problems and these may often be the most important. When they realize that the problems exist they have already been hurt by them. So first you must have a point of view which will help you. We have to sensitize ourselves to our surroundings so well that we know when to act.

In doing so we face a moral problem too. You can see that if you act within the framework you may not be doing all you can to prevent a bad trend. On the other hand if you act to prevent a trend, outside forces may catch up with you. If you can get this concept clearly in mind you will not worry so much about these moral questions which inevitably arise. You must operate your business in such a way so that it can be successful. Even though you have to do things in your business that seem to encourage bad trends, you must do so without hesitation to insure the future of your company. Yet on your free time you should work and plan to take action which will prevent this bad trend. Sometimes you will have to ring door bells, meet with citizens' committees, serve in the local government, and cooperate with civilian agencies in order to try to develop an atmosphere which is more conducive for your business. By acting in this way, I believe you will not be bothered by your contradictory actions.

My pattern for successful business leadership is simply this: act like a teacher and an educator. The best teaching is based on a good example and you must be able to set this example in order to help those with whom you live and work. To be a good teacher in business you must be able to understand this idea of framework. When the questions come up you must have something to articulate.

It is possible to detect a certain ambiguity in Doriot's use of the term "moral problem." While he does appear to place the company's "success" as a critical priority, there is clearly no advocacy of unethical acts to ensure that success. Certainly, the criminal acts we have seen in business of late would never merit his faintest approval. Indeed, Doriot would probably be the first to point out that such criminal acts almost always lead to degrees of corporate self-annihilation, not success.

INTERNATIONAL FRAME

Doriot's views on internationalism were probably among the most radical espoused by a Harvard Business School professor. What follows are the thoughts and ideas of a true "internationalist," even though (as you will see) he seems to have confused the whirling dervishes with dancers in India!

The international frame is the widest one for it seems to squeeze us from all sides. From now on we must merge our concepts of the international frame and the national one. When I was a boy in school I learned that if two containers were connected with a tube and partly filled, the fluid level would be the same in both. In the world we cannot have islands of plenty. Wars are only common denominators. I believe we are confusing communism and social evolution.

First we must determine what we want to do internationally. We export raw materials and we hope for areas in which we can invest capital, but most of all we want peace. You realize that it would be much easier for us to operate business within this country. We could probably maintain our standard of living and still exist comfortably without exports and imports. For the few raw materials that we do not find within our boundaries we could probably develop substitutes.

However, we must realize that transportation and communication have ruined our chances to live in such a secluded manner. They have made a connection between us and the rest of the world which is a two-way street. No longer will we be able to withdraw inside our boundaries and forget about the crazy world around us. What has brought us into a world where we cannot live in peace?

It is my opinion that this came about because we have handled international affairs on the same cheap, vote-getting rationale which we have used in domestic politics. We have permitted small men to run our government. These same small men have caused us much trouble abroad because foreign people cannot understand their tactics. When they treat foreign diplomats as they do politicians at home, the people in other countries are shocked and offended. They do not admire us for the way we act. Unfortunately, there is little chance that we will change from these policies. Most countries have their ablest men handling foreign affairs.

The number one worry for manufacturers is that wars pave the way toward nationalism and socialism. They force government participation in financing and regulating businesses. So, for the manufacturer's best interest he must find a way to insure peace. We pay more attention to the selection of a factory manager than to the choice of men handling our foreign affairs. We can no longer afford to treat such a serious problem so lightly.

There was a day when wars brought results. If we look at history we can see where one country used to gain the advantage over another because it had won a war. Now a country cannot benefit as it used to through a victory because of the rehabilitation work it must do in the conquered country and because of the internal adjustments brought on at home by the tremendous mobilization necessary to wage war.

I do not know of anyone who will say that World War III could prevent an increase in socialism. The chances are that it would bring more. We must realize that Russia does not fear war. I remember the statement of a Russian general in the late 1930s who said that out of World War I came Soviet Russia and that out of World War II would come Soviet Europe. With this attitude our competitor has no fear of the thing that might easily wreck us. His attitude is completely clear. We have no reason to be puzzled.

In business, you will find that the toughest competition comes from outside of your industry. You have some idea of what the competitors in your industry are doing. But those in other industries who do not speak your language and do not have the same problems that you do in procurement, production and labor, might easily create a product which will outsell yours and wreck you. This same situation exists internationally. We are now competing with people we do not understand. We speak different languages and we have very different backgrounds.

Another important distinction can be made about the world of today. In business, men compete but they still live together. I know very well that K.T. Keller, Chairman of the Board of Chrysler, does not get up in the morning either loving or hating Mr. Sloane who heads General Motors Corporation At work they compete against each other with all of their resources, but they also have lunch together and act very pleasantly toward each other in a social group. However, on the international scale we seem either to love each other or to hate each other. I think we have to learn to grow up and face other countries with the same tact, understanding, tolerance, and icy stare that we have toward our business competitors. We cannot have a great nation until we stop calling other people names.

We must put international relations on a higher plane. We have to look at the advantages and disadvantages of competing nations. Then without love or hate we must formulate a reasonable program. This applies to our policy towards the U.S.S.R. and to other nations as well.

As manufacturers you will have an influence on the people of your community. Men who work for you will come seeking advice. They will expect you to guide their thinking on international problems. Other businessmen will do the same. You may be on the school board and you will be active in civic projects. Many people will ask you about international affairs. Unless you are able to view world problems without being excited, you will not be able to help any of these people who seek your advice.

World War I was a man's war and not an equipment war. It was a very bloody struggle wherein many thousands of people were killed in a great battle within a few hours. After this costly war we quickly developed idealistic means to prevent another war. Out of this thinking came the plan to give the world democracy. The League [of Nations] was a very admirable project although [President Woodrow] Wilson's thinking was undoubtedly too advanced for the people of that time. However, all of us were too anxious with the progress of the new organization. Few people and nations actually tried to make it work. We gave up all hope that the League might solve some problems after it was unable to solve an initial few which were too much for its early capabilities. After this disappointment, selfish interests took over in many countries.

Just a few years later, Germany moved into the Saar Basin. How did this take place so soon after the end of World War I? Germany had been a republic and this republic failed. One of the primary causes for this failure was that we did not help Germany.

Inflation is fundamentally bad. Yet, in the first stages, many people benefit from it. Even though they will not admit, it, they gain from it. Then finally they find out that it is no good. You know in India they dance faster and faster so that they do not know what is happening. They have a wonderful time but they finally fall down. Inflation treats you the same way. Out of the confusion it causes, a strong man emerges. We can blame Hitler and the German people for all that happened but if we do, we must also blame ourselves for not correcting the conditions which made a Hitler inevitable. When Hitler came we could easily predict that World War II was just around the corner.

If some people had committed political suicide to fight for peace in 1938 we might have been able to do something about insuring it, but we were told that the public was not ready to make a stand at that time. Looking back, we cannot accept that answer. Nevertheless, the Japanese took care to see that the public was ready to fight World War II, and so we fought it.

By 1944, we began to get idealistic again, and we completely forgot the experience of twenty-five years ago. We must ask ourselves this question: Can we afford to spend resources and lives in a long hard war and then allow the planning to go to people who are complete novices? The United Nations organization is a good one as long as it is kept on a high plane. The same thing is true of the U.N. that was true with the League. It can accomplish some tasks effectively, but it is completely powerless to handle other ones. We will get a lot more out of the U.N. if we do not expect too much. With international organizations like the League and the U.N., the world is getting good experience. It is on this kind of experience with many disappointments and a few advancements that we must someday build a framework of world cooperation.

The Marshall Plan was a post-World War II effort by the United States aimed at reducing the hunger, homelessness, sickness, unemployment, and political restlessness of the 270 million people in sixteen nations in West Europe. The Marshall Plan was an admirable idea at the right time. Naturally, money was wasted, but for good reasons. You must understand that we have no experience in spending money in this way. It is very difficult to spend billions of dollars and make the spending purposeful. In fact you will find as you advance in business that it is as difficult to spend money wisely as it is to make money. So, we were handicapped with the Marshall Plan because we did not know how to distribute its benefits.

Furthermore, we were much too gentle when we administered the program. At one time I was asked to recommend a man for a job in the ECA. (The U.S. Department of State's Bureau of Educational and Cultural Affairs.) He was a General from the Army who had had an excellent record. Immediately I was told that he could not possibly be given the job because the Russians might object. Of course they will object if they can gain something by objecting. We must come to the place where we will be strong enough to develop a policy which we will follow.

Be cautious of your criticisms of the demagogue. Someone made him possible. Furthermore be very cautious of any new ideas. In these days it is hard to know what to believe and whom to believe. It is unfortunate that speech makers do not have to write their own speeches. It would be even better if a speech maker were forced to read a speech over again one year after he has made it. Personally, I would like to see legislation saying that no one law could be passed sooner than one year after it is proposed. If we had this kind of reflection we might have a better world. But unfortunately we insist on these things.

Because it is hard to know what to believe, you must know whom to believe. You have to look for men who do not want publicity. You must learn to trust the men who say what they think is right and not those who say what they think will make them popular. You must know who the false prophets are. You will have to read what they say.

In the paper we read about a big businessman who has sacrificed the best interests of his business to go to Washington for seven weeks to untangle some complicated problem. At the end of the seven weeks we see a letter from the president to the man, printed in the paper, congratulating him on the great service he has given to his country. Yet neither he nor the President nor the people know why he was there. Unfortunately, these false prophets have been the leaders of our country. They have represented our country to the world.

So you look at all of this and ask yourself: What can I do about this? Right now there is very little that you can do to change the world, so you must start to prepare yourself for the future. You must get a good background. You must seek to understand every important problem that comes up. To do this you will have to read and talk with people who can give you a sound point of view. After a while you will have a background which is good enough so that people will listen to you. Later, they will come to you for advice.

I have thought that we should have an Institute of Man. This would be a group of outstanding individuals who could evaluate the progress which Man has made. In light of this progress and the background of this progress this group could give some attention to the problems facing man today. From these people the country and its leaders could seek advice. But so far, no one has liked my idea and perhaps our leaders would not listen to such scholars even if the Institute existed.

As it is, now we are always about fifteen years behind. In business we realize that you cannot be fifteen years behind or you will go broke. But this is what we are trying to do in world affairs. Whether we like it or not, we are drifting towards a one-world concept. We do not want to be pushed into this world by others and we do not want to master it. We cannot exist as an island of plenty in a world of communism and socialism. We must stop this drifting by standing for something positive which will help other peoples to help themselves. We can help create one world which is peaceful and beneficial to all countries but still one which we do not dominate.

We must learn to operate on policy and not on expediency. In the future, life will be very miserable.unless we attempt to bring ourselves out of this dilemma which we currently face. You young men cannot say that you are unable to do anything. We do not know the answers to world problems but we must give them our deep and sincere interest. You must do better than men have ever done before.

Most of us who read the above in the context of the war in Iraq—the first big war of the twenty-first century—will find Doriot's words almost prophetic.

NATIONAL FRAME

With the 2004 U.S. presidential elections approaching, we may find considerable wisdom in what Georges Doriot had to say to his students on subjects related to manufacturing.

The related subjects have to do with government, and our choice of representatives, labor unions, bureaucrats, and our need to build pragmatic coalitions. Doriot begins to emerge less as a radical and more as a radical conservative.

This year we have an election coming up and we hear more lies and cheap politics. Why? We have this state of affairs because not long ago businessmen spent their summers in Maine and winters in Florida without thought of the communities from which they made all of their money. As a result, other people took an interest in politics and found that they could get money and benefits from doing so. The poor conditions today came directly from this start. We cannot lose interest in politics. We cannot afford to disregard the national frame because we think we cannot do something about it. The trends of recent history seem to be moving at an accelerated rate. Wars and depressions help to speed up these changes. Both are alike because both are costly and they both act as leveling agents. After you emerge from either kind, you find many people wanting what they never had. Now we face such a situation and we have been living under a government that promises to get these new things for people.

Work is not so important now as it used to be. Taxes are part of the reason for this, because the loss of incentive has eliminated part of the executive's interest in work. Also, we see much criticism of big business and this criticism causes the worker to lose interest in his work. Much of the objection to big business has come from educators and students. It seems to me that three factors have brought this about. Schoolteachers who have intelligence and ability naturally rebel against a society in which other men, fortunate enough to be in good business-es, can buy their wives fur coats and drive big Cadillacs. The teacher is further angered when the businessman tries to impress people with his material gains. Probably this is the seed of socialism because the teacher plans a new order, in theory, wherein these differentials need not exist.

Secondly, these ideas and resentments spread quickly to the work-ers. They have been prepared for a change by the promises of the theorists and educators. But these same planners do not realize that there is no standard for happiness. What hurts most is to be forced to give up something which you once had. It hurts most to give up a car, or to take your children out of school. It hurts to go back. Steady improvement pleases the most. This is what we should work for.

Finally, the teachers do not try to imagine what a man might be doing if he were not living in the machine age. It is easy enough to go into a factory and say that men should not be doing this or that and that we should provide more light, better conditions, and so on. But these often are goals we must work for and not immediate objectives. The only way you can judge a man's surroundings is to compare what he is doing with what else he otherwise might have been forced to do. Instead of working in a clean and healthy factory, a worker might be on a manure pile. Teachers do not realize what workers really want, so they cannot form a sound point-of-view. Without this, they incite trouble. Workers want most to work for a strong, hard man, whom they can admire and follow.

So teachers have sown the resentment of big business and this resentment has caused people to be less interested in hard work. Somehow we are losing the pride of workmanship.

After the turn of the century, everyone believed that size was the answer to all business ills. Any kind of a merger was considered a solution to the problems of each individual business. Look at many of our big companies and you find they got their start from such a combination.

Along with this, the bankers went wild without thinking. We had a period of easy money with much spending and no thinking. From my point of view, the bankers failed as much as any other class. At one time we had good bankers, trained mostly in Germany. Next to the minister, the banker had the greatest control over the welfare of the community. But as bankers permitted greater credit expansion without sound reasons, they paved the path towards failure and created a vacuum which the government had to fill. In 1928 when the president asked the bankers to help bring people to their senses, the bankers said any such statements by them would be selling the country short. In addition, all the experts went along with the racket. Remember this mistake of the bankers and do not let another group fail again. Sometimes to be right you must be alone. Sometimes you must make a great sacrifice to be right. But we are where we are today because too few businessmen would make that sacrifice.

So the market crashed and the Depression came. For the first time in the history of the country men did not have enough to eat. Always before, workers had had a little garden so that they could grow most of the food they needed. Now why had not people saved up for this eventuality? We had told them not to. We called saving old-fashioned. We lived in an age of materialism and shunned spiritual values entirely. So again, government took over.

This time, the capital of the United States moved from Wall Street to Washington. Before this, when a man wanted help, he went to the bankers in New York. Now he must go to Washington. The move came because New York did not act like a capital. I do not like nationalization or socialism. Yet I must admit that these movements develop only because we are not able to handle our own problems. So do not kick about these two evils because we fashioned them ourselves.

In this way we have gone from crisis to crisis. Please do not think that I am critical of the past and the men who shaped it. I am not critical, merely regretful. Try not to get the present modern habit of criticizing men of the past. Remember that standards have changed. Some of the former American businessmen were great Americans who made the great country in which you live. All that you have you owe to them. Who was the man who first operated factories for crippled men? Who paved the way for the $5 day? Who started to locate factories out in the country so that workmen could have nicer homes and he was that man often called a brute: Henry Ford. And we could outline similar great deeds of many other businesses of the past. So do not be critical of them. But in looking at the past, try to see the weaknesses of those who went before because these have given us the political framework in which we now live.

In today's world we have developed a progressive, materialistic society. We are envied by every other nation on Earth. This in itself should make you happy and proud, but you should also be modest. You must realize that other nations are often copying our weaknesses and not our strongest points.

Statistically, what kind of a nation do we have? In the last fifty years, we have increased the energy available per capita from 157 million BTUs to 233 million. We have increased the speed of our transportation machines from about 50 miles per hour to about 100; we own more than 36 million automobiles instead of 8,000; we use 33 million telephones instead of a little more than 1 million; we produce about four times as much steel, copper, almost fourteen times as much cement and about 200 times as much aluminum. Our population has doubled and national income has gone up about ten times. We shaved about 19 hours off of the normal workweek and increased life expectancy by almost 18 years.

So our record of materialism is quite outstanding. Yet measured in spiritual values, our record is not very good. Only recently have the schools and churches started to break down this materialistic society. We are beginning at last to teach people that things do not have to be expensive to be beautiful. But even though this materialistic record is not enough, your forefathers created a pretty good society with it. So you must have a feeling of modesty and with it the courage to try to do better. Mr. Eugene Meyer has stated this very well in his speech to the graduating class at Stanford this last June:

> And so I think it has come about in my time that the people of our country and of many other countries have made a resolve. It is not written in constitutions or party platforms but it is nevertheless a real and lasting resolve that the social cost of major depressions is too great a price to pay. That resolve is a dominating fact of our times; one that will shape much of the history that this graduating class will live through.

What are our problems today? First, we have a great increase in taxes. Now the tax rate is excessive. I do not like it primarily because it prevents giving. When you eliminate the possibility of doing for others, you take much away from life. This chance to do something for others has helped to make us a great people. Next, I do not like taxation because it almost forces the businessman to be immoral. In order to operate a business now you almost have to figure out ways of working the tax. To grow, you need profits. Yet often the profits after taxes, even in a good year, will not be big enough to finance that growth. Going farther and putting the business into an inflationary period, you often have a difficult time. To avoid this, you do all that you can to keep your business alive and to cut down on the taxes you must pay. We should not be forced to operate this way.

Finally, taxes make people afraid that money is being wasted anyway and we all take on the attitude of the bureaucrats. This is the form of indifference. It leads us to the conclusion that economy in government is not so important because we have an unlimited supply of funds anyway. This supposition sets up the quest for more security. If the state has unlimited funds, it can distribute unlimited welfare. The recent foreign spending has shown us that it is very difficult to spend money in large amounts efficiently. Government waste is contagious from one branch to another. We know that continued waste, high spending, and resulting taxes will only lead us along the road to constant devaluation.

Another major problem is the falling prestige of our government. Why is it that people speak of our great nation but of our poor government? Why will we insist on a great country and permit a weak, ineffective government? As future leaders you must be willing to work for better government. For if you will not, who else will shoulder the responsibility?

Many businessmen have forced the government to assume some of its present responsibilities because they have asked Washington to solve problems they should have worked out themselves. The government is not ready for the responsibility; so it organizes quickly. Rapid organization is generally ineffective and wasteful, but once established it is hard to do away with. Yet, after businessmen force responsibility onto the government and have to do what the government men say, they call it interference. Probably 98% of all the people going to Washington go with the hope of asking for something which they should not have. There is something in life in taking a beating but retaining a good conscience throughout. If you are not able to finance your business or handle your competitors, do not think that you must go to Washington for help. Businessmen must stand on their own feet and operate within the business community. Do not ask the government for help.

Make up your mind what you want out of the government. Then attempt to help your government work towards this goal. Say that government men are not paid well enough to attract men into the government service. I say that too many people in government get too much. Furthermore, we must develop some desire on the part of people to want to help their government and to desire to serve. Only by the interest of the people and by the desire of people to serve (and not profit by) the government can we hope to have a better government which operates closer to our wishes.

Closely allied with this falling prestige of government is the increase in government regulations. The only real worry about regulation is that it may favor one man over his competitors and that it may not be in force for sufficient time to make it understandable and workable. If every competitor is put in the same position by regulation, then it is not too hard to take.

Regulations are always assigned to take care of an extreme situation. Because of this, we need very able men to administer them justly. Without able men, the chances for justice through interpretation are not very good. Furthermore, it takes much time to train good men. We must attempt to do this. Nevertheless, our chances for training enough good men are not too good. For this reason, I think you as manufacturers have the responsibility for three kinds of action.

First, you must ensure that you do not act in such a way as to create the need for new legislation. We have brought on much restrictive legislation because we did not act in the best interests of society. After the legislation came, it covered many more issues than those in which business was harming the public interest. Secondly, you must put pressure on legislators to prevent the enactment of maximum laws to cover the maximum situation. You must talk down the need for legislation. Finally, you must help to get good legislation where it is necessary. The Securities and Exchange Commission is good now because a strong man in Boston was willing to go halfway in order to get good regulation.

We can only have good government and get good government service if we inject greater respect into what we do. We should have a government more like the English, where government service is one of the most respected of all careers. Poor administration of regulations means that we will get more legislation, not less. To stop bad trends, we must have good leadership. We will not have the leadership we need unless businessmen take an interest in government and make their services available to their government from time to time.

We see a major problem caused by changes in human desires and the growth of unions. From my standpoint, we must help to develop better leadership in unions and get better coordination between local and international organizations. Unfortunately, in this country we have encouraged the growth of huge international organizations which are politically powerful and potentially dangerous.

In theory, unions look good, but it is different when you get in a strike where workers might turn your car over or heave a brick through your window. It is different where, as recently happened in a Midwestern town, the union might threaten a strike if you did not hire back a man convicted on twelve counts of stealing from you. I am not a labor-hater but the other side of this question is very serious. Violence is not uncommon. Often you will get no help from the police or the federal government. If something goes bad, you have no one to whom you can turn for help.

In looking at the situation today, you must remember that we are where we are today, mainly because people were afraid of strikes. They were not strong. So they gave in to the unions and the unions grew on their successes. Too often employers worried about violence. I know this is difficult to face. Somehow you can protect yourself and you will, to get by when people threaten your life. But when they threaten your wife or your children, it is different. The only good result which can come from a threat comes when you are strong.

Labor is just helping us do a poor job. You must work for better conditions. You have to develop the strength and the qualities which you need to handle this situation. You have to develop contacts outside of your own labor relations man to advise you on labor affairs. He may be almost anyone. Some of the best advisers are newspapermen. You must be ready for this major challenge of facing the labor problem head-on.

In short, the national frame is the direct result of our own doing. We in turn will help shape the national frame of some years hence. You cannot put this challenge aside by thinking that you can do nothing about it. You need the desire and the interest to help. Added to that you must have the stamina and the drive to get in and in fact work towards the ends that you want.

Misguided though she may be, the little CIO girl who stands by the machine all day deserves credit for pushing doorbells and talking to voters half of the night. You have to counter her efforts with your own energy that is to be directed more intelligently. You must devote yourselves to three institutions in order for us to develop a society—your family, your community's schools, and your government. In doing so you will help to build a national framework which gives us a chance to do better work and live better lives.

TECHNOLOGICAL FRAMEWORK

The accelerated rate of history applies specifically to science. In order to adjust to technical evolution, you must, as a manufacturer, have a liking for, a feeling for, and an understanding of science. The technical frame is the hardest for us to understand. For this reason we forget to link the technical frame with the social. Many sociological disturbances are caused because of technical mistakes. In a day when we busy ourselves with human problems, we must keep this in mind.

Science is the unknown. You have a growth curve in science but it is impossible to extrapolate this curve. Only as you look back does it appear to be smooth. Many people want to know what will happen in science in the next ten years. In a day where it takes five to seven years from "test tube to tanker," as one chemical company has noted, and where it takes many years to train good workmen and foremen, you cannot predict what will happen in the immediate future with great accuracy. An important step may be possible technically but it will not develop for business reasons. So, in this frame, we work in an area of unknowns.

You must realize that every day many people are working hard to make obsolete all that you have done so far. If you have invested a lot of money in a big, new plant, you have to understand that before it is complete the scientists will have started to work on projects which might make this plant almost worthless.

Furthermore, in this area you must think about the problem of how much leadership you should have in the field of research. Should you be first, last, just behind the leader or where? To this question, there is no standard reply. Companies have failed and also achieved great successes in each position.

With these two problems as background, you must develop a sensitive but cold-blooded feel for scientific developments in your field. You must read and study to develop this feel. At first you will have to work on things which you do not even understand. In time you will be able to sort out the things which are important; you will have some idea what you should look for in the future.

This feel cannot be the scientific understanding of what is going on or how new ideas have been developed. Rather it must be an insight into the possible significance of these new ideas. You can have a scientific feel for the facts and yet not be ready to gamble on their business implications.

When you work with things you do not understand, then you will have to go to technical people to get help. You should spend a full evening every two weeks, either alone or with a group of friends, discussing new scientific developments. You must use this time in order to get a feel. But do not rely on scientists or technical people to help you size up the business implications of new findings. I worry more about the engineers and technical men in this area than I do the men with broad backgrounds. The business feel is something which you yourself must develop.

Remember that the thing which kills you in business is uncertainty. To prevent uncertainty in the field of technological evolution, you must have a hunch about these new developments. In the field of science, you cannot predict. You cannot aim at a definite goal. You can only have the sense of direction. It is one thing to exercise good judgment on what you know. Most of us can deal with the problems we see. It is quite another task to handle adequately those problems we do not know about, those new developments which make our plant and equipment out-of-date and which come upon us as a complete surprise. Here you cannot afford to be overtaken because surprise is death without a struggle. You must have the feel for science in order to give yourself the time to handle the problems which new developments will surely bring.

SEEKING ADVICE

Today, running a business is very hard because all of the frames affect us. There was a time when we only had to deal with the problems inside of the company. This made operating much easier because you could concentrate on situations immediately facing you, and did not have to worry about problems almost completely beyond your control. This situation no longer exists because we have now used up many of our raw materials, and we do not have expanding new markets for the future. Because it is difficult to operate a business in this day you must learn to use the help and guidance of other people and you must develop a way of choosing the men from whom you get advice. There is a real difference between help from an employee and help from someone outside. To do well you need the help of both groups. At this point we should consider the problems in seeking outside advice—when you should have it and how often you should ask for it. You must consider advice as a tremendous lever. It will either work for you or against you. One of your most important tasks will be to select men to help you.

Bankers

The most common thing we need is money. At a time when the means of capital accumulation are changing radically, the problem of finding capital will probably be the hardest one that you will face. To get capital you must have credit. You should never have to go after capital because the minute you do the cost of capital goes up and it shies away from you. The important prerequisite is personal credit.

Personal credit is very hard to define but it is a mirror of your thoughts, actions, and accomplishments. It must result from your personal success as an individual—as a father, husband, neighbor, a man living with understanding and discretion. It can be made or destroyed by many small things: being on time or late; by being kind or unkind at a particular time; by your action toward employees; by the activities of your family; by your conduct on the golf course; by the letters that you answer and the ones that you forget to answer. Five years ago a record was started with your name on it. The record is like a tape recorder which follows closely at your heels to observe and record all that you do. There is no way you can change the story of your past or how it is recorded in the future. From now on it is your job to make that record so good that the keenest observer can look at it at any time and find it perfect.

Company credit is built on your personal record. The character of a corporation must be reflected through its people. Without good personal credit you will be unable to build credit for your company. You must acquire habits so that you do not have to worry about your record. Remember, you do not go after capital but it seeks you out.

The most common source of funds for you is the commercial bank. So, from now on one of your problems is to make friends with the commercial banker. Borrowing money is not quite like buying an ice-cream soda. Do you remember the story of Antonio in front of the Chase National Bank?

Antonio had a pushcart from which he sold peanuts. He always parked it in front of the Chase Bank. One day his friend, Pete, said to him, "Antonio, loan me a nickel."

Antonio said, "No, I can't."

"Why?" asked Pete.

Antonio pointed to the big bank in back of him and said, "You see that building?" "Sure."

"Well," said Antonio, "we made a deal."

"Oh?"

"They don't sell peanuts; I don't loan money."

When you get turned down you will understand what this story means. I can remember the day when I wanted to borrow $10,000,000 for a company. That was back in the days when a dollar was a real dollar. Well, we left the sidewalk, went to the 24th floor, presented our story, and returned to the sidewalk. It took us only three minutes. Getting turned down makes you feel pretty bad. Worst of all, once you are turned down your credit is badly hurt and everybody knows it. Somehow, bankers compete with each other but still each one always knows what the other one does.

One time I went to the Midwest to borrow money. I had an appointment for 9:00 a.m., so I got there a little early and walked to the president's office. There I met a distinguished and intelligent man. I started to talk with him, hoping to make the kind of impression I thought I would need in order to borrow the money. After a few minutes the man politely dismissed himself and said he had other things to do. Only then did I learn that he was actually the president's assistant. Yet, knowing him did help me at that bank. When I go there now I always try to stop and see him. This merely illustrates that in building credit little things—insignificant things—can count a great deal.

It will be impossible for you to borrow money at the time you need it unless you have been able to foresee that need. If you need money you never thought you would need, you are a washout. You must first build up a relationship with the banker so that he trusts you and then you must have laid the groundwork for borrowing on the basis of wise forecasts. The man who cannot forecast needs is not the kind of man in whom the bankers will put a great deal of trust.

First, let us look at what the banker wants. He would like to have you deposit money in his bank in the form of pure gold. He would like not to pay you any interest on the money, and after a long period of having the money deposited in the bank he would like to loan you a small portion of it, particularly at a high rate of interest and with absolute security.

And what does the manufacturer want? He would like to have any amount of money anytime without interest and without security. In addition, he would like to be able to borrow without telling anybody why he wants the money.

Naturally, both these points of view are extremes. We need to bring the two points of view together in a working arrangement. Remember that the banker deals only in reputation. He must work in such a way so that his reputation is safeguarded. Besides being honest, he must have the ability to get money back with a reasonable return. Such is the banker's position. Your relationship with him must be one in which the honeymoon does not end.

Money comes in different grades just like milk. All money looks the same just as all milk looks the same, but in both there are differences in quality. What you want is Grade A money. One time a man went to see Baron Rothschild, the old financier of Frankfurt, Germany, and asked to borrow some money. The Baron said, "I will not loan you the money but I will walk with you arm in arm across the floor of the exchange." In doing so, of course, he helped the man tremendously.

In New York, a bank was being reorganized. J.P. Morgan did not take part in the reorganization nor did he give the bank his active support. All he did was to take out some time during the noon hour one day and walk over to the new bank. He dropped in, looked around very casually, and then strolled back to his office. Yet his contribution to the later success of the bank may have been as important as that of any other man.

People take a great interest in the loans of banks. Remember the old French proverb: "Tell me what company you keep and I will tell you who you are." If you can keep the bankers and if you can get their financial support then you are getting Grade A money.

The good banker can loan you money but he can also help you in many other ways. He has a breadth of contacts which you do not have. He talks to other bankers, to men in a wide variety of activity. He meets people with a point of view that you may never get. He has a feel for the money market and for the business condition of the country. He gets interesting opinions on our political framework. Finally, he knows the people from whom you buy and to whom you sell. In many ways, therefore, his help and guidance are worth much more than the money he is able to loan.

Your relationship with the banker should be handled in such a way so that you talk freely with him about all of your problems. If you discuss your affairs carefully with him you may never have to talk to him about money. Then, how do you pick him? The large bank has the advantage of a greater legal loaning limit. Furthermore, the large banker usually has better contacts and wider relationships. For the intangibles you receive along with the money you borrow, the large bank has the advantage.

Some people say that if you are small you should go to a small bank. In some respects this may be true but generally you can get the same type of service from a large bank if you get acquainted intimately with a good loan officer who trusts you and who is trusted by the top man. Here your relationship must be a dual one. You must be able to work with the loan officer but you must also be respected by the top man so that the loan officer can get for you what you want. Taking the advantages and disadvantages of size into account, I say that you should try to get a larger bank. In some cases the smaller bank may be satisfactory, but generally I would advise you to seek the larger one.

Remember this rule: You cannot change banks. Banking is a closed community. At the outset you must choose a good banking organization. A great deal depends on this. I remember in the early '20s in Cleveland there were two banks. One was housed in a big, beautiful, impressive building—at that time the largest bank building in the world. The other bank was across the street in quarters not nearly so comfortable. But as the two banks were much different in appearance so they were managed by different types of men. When the Crash came the beautiful bank, the Union Bank closed its doors in complete failure. The dingy one across the street, the Cleveland Trust Company, kept its doors open so that each depositor could draw out his money. The Cleveland Trust Company operated throughout the Depression and today it is still one of the leading banks of the country. It is important for you to pick the right bank at the outset. (The Cleveland Trust continues to operate in 2004.)

If you get a good banker now you will not be able to measure the credit in dollars but you will reap it in dividends later. You must start preparing today for the time when you will need credit. Once you have selected your bankers you must tell them the truth. You may be able to bluff other people but you cannot do so with your banker. Try to operate by this rule: Let him get the good news about you from someone else; always see to it that he hears the bad news from you first. This rule is inflexible. Furthermore, do not wait for bad news to come but warn him if it seems to be approaching. Another rule is equally inflexible: Never let your banker see you when you are not in complete mastery of yourself and your faculties. The easiest way to destroy much of the credit you have been able to build is to let your banker see you when you are drunk, saying things you should never be saying. You must also figure out a way to give him systematic reports of your progress. It is your third important rule to keep him posted in such a way that he is able to view your needs and also to see that you are businesslike in your relationship with him.

When you get big you will need big banks. When this time comes do not dump your local banker. Spread out your deposits with a number of banks. Large corporations like Chrysler have deposits in banks all over the country. This can help you in many ways. Reciprocity is important. It would be very poor taste to forget the man who originally gave you your start.

In selecting an investment banker you do not buy money but you buy the name. The good name is worth a great deal. You can always borrow money in this country, but again you will need much more than this. The investment banker has only one thing to sell and that is reputation. I would much rather have a $500,000 issue from Morgan or Kuhn Loeb than a $2,000,000 issue from an unknown house. These substantial houses are where they are because their judgment was superior. People buy new issues on the basis of the banking name as often as they do on the basis of your company name. Once you get money from a good house you will probably have an easier time with suppliers, in your sales, and in all of your other relationships in business.

If you are a small company, you may have to go to a banker. But I say, go to the largest firm that will take you. Here again you should find a firm and stick with it. The New York firms are usually the best for originating. They can generally do you the most good and they are, for the most part, in the best position to offer you intangibles.

Generally, I would rather not have my banker on the board of directors. You still want some independence from the banker even though he knows all about you. Putting him on the board tends to make him think that he owns the business. I would rather not have him cultivate this feeling. With a banker on the board there is always the problem of removal. Once you put him on the board you will have a very difficult problem if you want to take him off of it. Do not get into this kind of a trap. All human relations start with a honeymoon. They may end in tragedy. If you do put a banker on your board be very careful that you do so with your eyes open.

The insurance companies today have more and more to invest. They are large enough to absorb entire issues so often they go directly to the company instead of negotiating with investment houses. For the manufacturer this is sometimes unfortunate because you can generally get more assistance from the investment banker than you can from an insurance company.

The head of the business generally cannot take care of the daily surveillance of financial matters. He must put the responsibility in the hands of another whom he can trust and with whom he can work effectively. Then the president must be careful to see that he is informed by his treasurer and that he uses the information carefully. He must always say the right thing.

Bill Knudsen, the Danish immigrant who became the great production man, was indicted by the New Deal in the 1930s. Because he was a naturalized immigrant who had worked very hard for this country, he was greatly disappointed by the indictment. Nevertheless, when the war broke out Franklin Roosevelt called him to Washington to ask him to become chief of the OPM (Office of Production Management for the U.S. War Department which was responsible for transforming general production into wartime production). Returning to Detroit, Mr. Knudsen was asked by his colleagues how he got along in his conference with the president. He pointed to a swordfish mounted on a plaque on the wall and muttered: "Do you know why he's there? He opened his mouth at the wrong time!" Remember this story when you are about to talk inappropriately.

Do not think that operating a company is operating a factory. You must broaden your concept far beyond this. Business is the art of spending money wisely.

Auditors

The next source from which you will seek advice is the auditor. In going to the bank you must always have enough information. You must study your business so carefully that you will know exactly the facts which your banker might like to have. Do not get caught in need of information which you do not possess. It is up to you to know what they might need at any time. But the figures you show them should be checked. It is not that the banker will not trust you, but it is good practice in banking to have figures checked by someone who is reliable. For this you need a good auditor.

When you select an auditor you expect to get a certain amount of standing. This standing will eventually show up in your relationships with the banks. Standing, like credit, must seek you out. Therefore, it is best if you take a national firm. Here you cannot take chances. There are many arguments in favor of a small firm. Yet how can you be sure that the top man in a small firm is better than a third or fourth man in a large one?

Furthermore, you want help beyond the mere auditing work that you get. You should be able to get advice on taxes, personnel, and on a wide variety of problems. You want someone who can talk to you and dig into your worries. Do not think that you are hiring someone merely to do an audit. When you select an auditor you are buying advice.

If your auditor trusts you, he will back you up. If he does not, he will be extraordinarily cautious. You cannot try to slip anything over on him. Remember he is the one who sees you completely naked. It is very hard to tell your auditor how beautiful you are. But, your auditor is your tailor. He dresses you up so that you look good to other people. He can go to the bank for you and back you up.

Lawyers

When you seek advice you are really carrying a flag. On the flag is written the names of the advisers: your commercial banker, your investment banker, your auditor. Now we will add the name of your lawyers.

A doctor, lawyer, and a priest were shipwrecked and landed on a small island. The next day they saw a larger island about a mile away and drew lots to see who should go. The lawyer was thereby chosen. While swimming, two sharks attacked him. The priest prayed and the doctor took a sedation. However, the sharks stayed alongside the lawyer as he swam to the big island and as he returned. When the lawyer came up on the beach both friends were amazed and asked: "Why didn't the sharks eat you?" "Oh," said the lawyer, "professional ethics."

Today, business is so complicated that you have to sleep with a lawyer, eat with another, and then hire a third to check on the first two. In the days of reorganization we needed lawyers badly. They were the only ones who could guide the company that had reorganized. But now we are getting into a world in which almost everything we do has legal connotations. You must have legal advice in order to be safe in business. First, we must incorporate and you have to know what state laws are best for you. Next, you have to determine what is the best kind of borrowing for you to do. This all takes legal counsel. Add to this the many laws and the interpretation of these laws which you must know in order to operate. It does you no good to know the patent law unless you know the new interpretations taken by the courts on the law in the last twelve years.

Unfortunately, however, I know of no profession where you find greater extremes in professional conduct. On the one extreme you find great men like Stimson who was an outstanding leader in our government. Yet from the same school and classes you will find men with absolutely no respect and responsibility: men who do not see the difference between justice and winning a case.

It reminds me of the story in which St. Peter and Satan had arranged to share the expenses of maintaining a wall between Heaven and Hell. One day the wall crumpled and Satan did not want to have it fixed. He argued that it did not particularly benefit him to have such a separation. However, St. Peter could not put up with it. So he went ahead and had the wall fixed and sent Satan the bill. Satan would not pay. Thereupon St. Peter said that he would sue Satan. At this, Satan replied, "How can you? I've got all the lawyers." Silly as this story is, it is still pretty relevant.

Since you will be judged by the company that you keep, you must pick the kind of a lawyer that will give you integrity in the eyes of others. Do not compromise on reputation. Remember that business is not one man in a canoe without a current to worry about. It is a ship with many men who need many navigational aids to get through turbulent waters. In today's turbulent waters you must have a tough-minded counsel, so you must look for good firms, the kind that will not take a crook for a client. You do not want a man who is like you, but you want a man who understands you. Do not pick a man who always wants a fight because this will cost you money. Remember, too, that it will be better to have a lawyer meet with the board of directors

Also, counsel is often used on nonrecurring problems, principally because ideas from an outsider are better accepted. The outsider is expendable. For this reason he can suggest something that the president has in mind, and the president can still say that it is the idea of the consultant and not his own. This could be a great advantage in attempting to sell something to the directors which is for the good of the company but which would look suspicious if originating from the president.

Often it takes the opinion of an outsider to help sell securities. Security buyers have been known to accept the opinion of a consulting engineer or an industrial designer or a marketing-research organization when they would not accept the same ideas from company executives. This is especially true on new stock issues.

In this context, I would like to give you a classification of individuals which should serve only as a guide to help channel some of your ideas. In no way should you consider it a fixed framework but rather as an aid in helping you understand some of the people you will meet in business. During the course of the year I have been trying to help you to become an operating man. In business I think you will find three types: promoters, advice-givers, and operators.

The promoter has a great deal of imagination and he is able to look ahead. He gets many new ideas and he is very good at selling them. However, he generally will not concern himself with daily happenings and problems. The term, "promoter," should not have a cheap connotation. These qualities are very desirable and essential in the conception of new ideas and in putting them into initial action. The trouble sometimes occurs when a promoter tries to become an operating man. The operator has many qualities similar to those of the promoter but they are in a lesser degree. Coupled with these is the quality to take a job and to stay with it until the problems are solved and the operation is running smoothly. Then he has to stick with it day after day to see that it continues to run smoothly.

The third man, the advice-giver, generally fails as an operator and as a promoter. He performs brilliantly in thinking out the problem. He can handle it in the finest detail and he can explore every facet of it carefully and intelligently, yet the edge generally goes to the good operating man, the one who can do so well at carrying out a plan to successful completion.

Today, however, we are concerned with the advice-givers. I want to give you a passage about business which I think is very carefully stated:

> The greatest trust between man and man is the trust of giving counsel; for in other forms of confidences men commit parts of their life, their lands, their goods, their children, their credit, some particular affair; but to such as they make their counselors they commit the whole; (by how much the more they are obliged to all faith and integrity). The wisest need not think it any diminution to their greatness or derogation to their sufficiency to rely upon counsel. The inconveniences that have been noted in calling and using counsel are three. First, the revealing of affairs whereby they become less secret; secondly, the weakening of the authority of men as if they were less of themselves; thirdly, the danger of being unfaithfully counseled, and more for the good of them that counsel than of him that is counseled. The true composition of a counselor is, rather to be skillful in their master's business than in his nature, for he is likely to advise him and not to feed his humor.

This sounds pretty up-to-date, doesn't it? But it was written by Francis Bacon in 1597. I merely took the liberty of putting in the word "man" where Bacon had written "princes." From now on you must be aware of this very important trust of giving advice. Counsel-asking and counsel-giving are now daily jobs in your life. I hope that you will not have to give too much counsel before you are a little older and more experienced. Nevertheless, I know you will have to seek counsel from this time on. Your problem is to learn how to ask for it.

Consultants

In consultants you find many men who have no modesty. Most of them operate on the assumption that they can analyze your business immediately. We know that some day you will need somebody's advice on something. I think we have to go on the theory that there is a good man to solve your problem in some firm somewhere, but you can never afford to face the problem of choosing between firms. This is the most important rule in seeking counsel. You must take a different point of view. You must find out who in the firm is good at particular problems. Then you go to him. Do not be sold a bill of goods by a single firm. Rather seek out the man. In order to do this you must be aware of the kind of work done by various men in the consulting field. Certainly you must be aware of this long before you are faced with the problem on which you need advice. If you can do this and prepare yourself for the future, then you will be ready to seek the specific man.

Consulting firms do not specialize because it does not seem to pay off. As a result each firm claims that it can do almost anything. It is easy to see that this cannot be the case. Your plan should be to go to the firm and say that you will hire them if they will give you the services of the man you want. If you can do this, you will not be bothered by the problem of choosing between firms. The only time when it makes no difference what firm you pick is when you have the problem of getting professional advice in order to sell an idea to someone on the outside.

Remember there is nothing more wasteful and expensive than spending time to get information which has already been gathered at someone else's expense. Be the kind of businessman who knows where to go for information. Do not be the one who knows everything because, of course, that is very dangerous. Be the one who knows where he can find what he needs.

The greatest cost for the consultant is in soliciting. This requires a psychology which often results in giving the president the kind of a report he wants to get. Very few consultants give reports which are completely honest.

Today I would like to tell you the story of one firm's experiences with engineering consultants. The McKeesport Tin Plate Company had a record in the mid-1930s which made it the country's most successful tin-plate manufacturer. The company bought steel bars from the U.S. Steel Company and rolled these into plates, which were later coated with tin. The tin plates were sold to ten can-making companies in the United States. McKeesport sold to the National Can Company, the third-largest can company, and also to its competitors.

During the 1930s, the steel companies learned to make continuous rolled steel plate. From that point it was very easy for them to tin it and ship it to the can companies. The U.S. Steel Company built a big plant just three miles from McKeesport in 1936, and this plant made the McKeesport plant completely obsolete. At this point the stockholders of McKeesport began to get worried and asked a very reliable consulting firm for a report. The consultants said that McKeesport was in sound financial shape and that the only possible trouble was that some of their equipment was out-of-date. In truth, most of their investment was tied up in rolling equipment which was now practically worthless. In addition, the consultants stated that the swing to fully mechanical rolling was merely a vogue and that the trend in the future would come back, so that McKeesport was not in as bad shape as some people supposed.

The real trouble which the consultants did not indicate was that the profit in making tin plate does not come from changing the bar to the roll but in the tinning. Because of this the steel companies wanted to turn out tin plate rather than steel bars as an end-product. Nevertheless, the stockholders were content with the engineers report and they let the matter go for a year and a half. By that time the steel company had made the decision to cut off the supply of steel bars to McKeesport. In addition, McKeesport began to lose some of its clients. National Can, of course, had to buy from McKeesport and it was being hampered by the arrangement. Both companies started to lose money. At this time the board was reorganized and three new directors were brought in.

Now, what do you do in a situation like this? The answer is simple enough. You make everyone think that what you have is worth something. McKeesport had a good reputation and a good list of clients. The directors had to make this organization look like a strong competitor and hope that someone would want to buy it. So the management was reorganized and one of the new directors became the operating head of the company.

In order to convince the stockholders a new engineering consulting firm came in to make a new report. The new report stated that McKeesport was completely lost with the old type of equipment and that National Can also would be lost if it had to continue to buy tin plate from the parent company. The conclusions of the two reports completely contradicted each other. Both consulting firms were highly regarded. The moral of this story is quite clear: By going to a good firm and spending a great deal of money you do not necessarily get good advice. Well, the new management bolstered up the tin-plate company to the point where it began to look strong and then one of the steel companies finally bought it. So the story has a much more fortunate outcome than it might have had if the stockholders had continued on the advice of the first consulting firm.

So, what do you do about seeking consulting advice? You must hire consultants to write only one report. Make it clear at the outset that there will be no repeat business. Do not keep them on a retainer. In the first McKeesport report the consultants clearly indicated that another report probably would be necessary to study the rolling machinery. On a one-shot basis this would never have been possible. Only on the arrangement of one report can you expect to get wise counsel.

Repeat business may be satisfactory where you can measure the results attained by the consultants' work. However, in most cases it is very difficult to measure results. In these cases you must clearly state at the outset of the agreement that you are engaging the firm to make a study and that this is the last time you will ask them for their help.

From now on you will seek counsel. You must learn how to do that. It takes a great deal of practice to ask for advice. You must know how to prepare yourself for this. Whenever you come to someone to ask for something you must be prepared for the situation. Too often young people do not know how to prepare themselves. From now on counsel-seeking is one of your most important responsibilities. Learn how to do it well.

Finally, I would like to talk about the people who help you form a successful connection between your company and your public. In this sketch you will see the two-way relationship between your organization which makes a product and delivers it to the people who buy the product.

You will find, however, that the public does much more than buy your product. Most of them think and all of them believe that they think. Because of this they can have attitudes towards you. Oftentimes many more people will use your products than will buy them. Because of this your relationship with your consumer may be very satisfactory, but if it is not good with the final user then you may lose sales. Furthermore, the public is your potential labor force. Some members of the public are your employees. Finally, some of the public own your business. So the connection of your company with the public is not a simple one. To make it successful you will probably need the help of experts in the field of industrial design, advertising, publicity, and public relations.

THE INVESTOR

I N T H E I N T R O D U C T I O N to the 1971 annual report for
American Research & Development, a section that General
Georges Doriot took great interest in personally writing, the
following appears:

1971 was ARD's 25th year of operation. During the life of ARD
certain things have taken place:

- The investment community became interested in venture capital. As
speculative excesses increased, understanding and interest tended
to disappear. Disillusions and disenchantment usually follow periods
when the true meaning of a task is ignored and forgotten.

- Venture capital seems to have shifted from a constructive, difficult
task to a new method of speculation.

- Capital gains have become a primary goal instead of being considered as a reward for a constructive task well done.

- Manufacturing capital gains seems to be of more importance than
manufacturing products. As a matter of fact, in many cases the
latter seems to be of little importance!

Doriot died in 1987, well before the Internet bubble of the 1990s. But he may well have been writing about the state of venture capital in 2002.

More than any of the present-day academics and experts who theorize about venture capital, Doriot understood the dialectic of the term. Venture capital is an economic development tool that not only has the ability to construct businesses and jobs, but also provide extraordinary financial returns to those who chose to use it. At the same time he recognized the danger that venture capital could be used purely as a transactional financial instrument, almost to the detriment of its overall development role.

Investing venture capital in a company in return for an equity stake was nothing unique by the time American Research & Development came on the scene in 1946. The Rockefellers, the Whitneys and the Rosenwalds already were investors in such companies as McDonnell Douglas and Eastern Airlines. But it was Doriot who codified the process at ARD. Here's how he described ARD's method of operation:

American Research & Development Corporation

- assists in creating companies based on the ideas and techniques of competent men

- invests in new companies

- invests in existing small or medium-sized companies which appear to have growth potential

In addition to supplying capital, ARD makes available to companies the technical and administrative experience of its management, board of directors and its many advisers in the United States and abroad. There is no single industry or group of industries into which ARD's funds are directed. Many of the investments are in technically based companies, but funds also have been invested in such diverse fields as publishing, but funds also have been invested in such diverse fields as publishing, entertainment, consumer goods, communications, educational supplies and equipment, and consulting and data-processing services. Investment opportunities in any field of endeavor which is felt to be constructive and to possess exceptional possibilities for growth are to be considered.

ARD seeks an equity position or its equivalent in all ventures. It provides long-term capital, incurring the risks and realizing the gains that accrue from such a policy. ARD has no specific formula for financing projects. Each investment opportunity is considered separately, and the form of participation is designed to meet the individual requirements of the situation. The underlying principle in formulating an investment agreement is that the greatest ultimate success will result when the arrangements are regarded as equitable and satisfactory by all the parties concerned.

The amount of capital which ARD invests in a single situation is flexible and, again, is determined by the client's requirements. The participation by the management of the portfolio company in the ownership of the company is considered to be of great importance to its growth. In some cases, ARD may seek the support of other financial groups, with the agreement of all parties, because the association of additional and constructive investors is often considered to be in the best interests of a company's development.

ARD does not seek control in the companies in which it invests; however, there are situations where the amount of capital required and the degree of risk involved may necessitate that ARD have a controlling interest during the company's early years. Even in such cases, ARD does not manage companies. ARD seeks to invest only in situations where able management by men of competence and integrity seems assured.

The statement of mission and purpose wasn't simply boilerplate that was attached to the beginning of each annual report that ARD published. Doriot firmly believed in these principles and demanded that those who worked at ARD always guide their practice by these principles.

Early venture capitalists, the founders of such funds as Kleiner Perkins Caufield & Byers, the Mayfield Fund, and TA Associates, recall early discussions with institutional investors, especially those that managed university endowments and the assets of wealthy individuals. And it always was about the ability to create a new economy out of the vast wealth of knowledge and research that lay within the walls of universities and research organizations. There also was the understanding that growth could come only from the ability to spawn new undertakings.

These were ideas that Doriot himself had preached at the end of World War II. And it was this vision that Ralph Flanders, the first president of ARD and a co-founder along with Doriot, espoused.

> The postwar prosperity of America depends in a large measure on finding financial support for the comparatively small percentage of new ideas and developments which give promise of expanded production and employment, and an increased standard of living for the American people. We cannot float along indefinitely on the enterprise and vision of preceding generations.
>
> To be confident that we are in an expanding, instead of a static or frozen economy, we must have a reasonably high birthrate of new undertakings.

The formation and the structure of American Research & Development in 1946 was a seminal event, not because it created a new venture-capital fund, but because it established a set of practices that until then had been very much an extemporaneous practice. Doriot didn't try to create a set of absolute criteria. Indeed, he clearly emphasized that each deal was unique and would be evaluated on its own merits.

> The Company does not have the advantage of conducting its business on the basis of measured physical assets. Statistical analysis, ratio analysis, are often of little value in this type of business. Men and ideas are our assets. Their measurement and evaluation are our problems.

At the same time he was quick to reassure entrepreneurs that ARD would never seek to operate or manage the company, even when the financing might involve owning a majority stake. It was important to Doriot that entrepreneurs trusted their financiers as sources of capital and not see them as threats to their management and ownership of their enterprises.

In the late 1960s, we are told, the CEO of Xerox Corporation visited Doriot, whose ARD was the largest shareholder of DEC, to make a pitch for DEC. "Why talk to me? I am only an investor. I don't control the company or run it on a day-to-day basis," Doriot said. And the Xerox honcho unbelievingly pointed out that Doriot's ARD owned nearly two-thirds of DEC's outstanding shares. "If that isn't control, what is?" But Doriot persisted that DEC was Ken Olsen's company and all discussions about a sale would have to be directed to Ken Olsen. Miffed, the Xerox head walked out. Soon after, Xerox purchased Scientific Data Systems for nearly $1 billion.

For Doriot, the goal was to build companies in a "constructive" way. And he was willing to acknowledge the need of others—partners—in achieving the goal. Indeed, he was operating at a time when the idea of young companies going public to provide liquidity to investors and managers was unknown. Constructing a company was a deliberate and systematic process and the company's own managers were the ones best equipped to handle it.

At the end of the first year of operations, Doriot wrote:

> With reference to investments, it is quite early to make definitive forecasts. These young, promising companies are passing the normal difficult periods of early growth. It is hoped that their managements will grow with their businesses and assimilate the different and new problems and worries brought forth by increased size.
>
> Their problems of today are typical of the times; and it may be difficult for some people, accustomed as they are to reading of easy sales and increasing industrial profits, to realize that a period like the

present creates many difficulties in the building of a new company. Raw materials are sometimes not readily available to someone who is not an old client. A dollar does not "build" as much as one would like it to. These problems and others can be met only with hard work and assistance from friends.

Generally speaking, it can be stated that the hopes on the basis of which investments made are still there. Their realizations in some cases are on schedule; in other cases they are delayed. As always, realizations cost more and take longer than expected. Setting high goals stimulates ability, the fact that they are not always reached quickly suggests patience.

Over the years many have argued that venture capital is a uniquely American phenomenon. It works because of the free-enterprise system, because of the cultural propensity among Americans to push the envelope and because the stock markets had a greater willingness to finance innovation and risk. Certainly, most of venture capital's gains have come within the framework of the U.S. economy and because of the generous valuations that the markets have given new companies.

Doriot didn't see venture capital as a purely American phenomenon. Indeed, in the aftermath of the formation of ARD, he began talks to launch similar enterprises in Canada and Europe.

One talks about Europe, but one must remember that "Europe as such" is still a nebulous entity made up of different and divergent parts, which may not come or stay together unless private and government relationships are created in a constructive and desirable way to the point where disengagement becomes desirable and difficult. The possibility of a general monetary business recession should not be overlooked. However, timing loses some of its importance if the goal is certain and a long-range outlook is taken.

In the years after the First World War, although he already had moved to the U.S., he kept on looking at what was happening in France. He followed the impact of the Dawes Plan—the blueprint for

Post-World War I reconstruction—and argued that it punished not just Germany but France as well. And he quickly began to talk about the values of economic policies and programs that would encompass entire communities, not single nations.

Forming a European venture-capital organization together with a Canadian one and an American one was a natural evolution of Doriot's thinking.

Although the world was fragmented economically at the time Doriot envisaged the formation of the European and Canadian versions of ARD, he clearly recognized some of the key issues behind their formation and growth. He recognized the need for U.S. companies to seek markets and allies abroad, especially in technology-related businesses. He also seemed to realize that companies in Canada and in Europe needed access to the U.S. markets in order to gain credibility and to grow to be significant companies.

But there was a hitch. Entrepreneurship and entrepreneurial cultures in both Europe and Canada were unformed. And funding the infrastructure that would help support the venture-capital effort and the development of entrepreneurial businesses was going to be an extremely difficult proposition.

The Canadian venture fund came first. And its chairman, A. Bruce Matthews, described the fund thusly:

> At this stage in the development of our Canadian economy it is important to encourage imaginative and progressive men with new ideas and with new concepts to create and build successful enterprises and thereby expand production and employment. Perhaps never before in our history has it been so important that Canada make good and effective use of its human resources.
>
> Canadian Enterprise Development Corporation Limited (CED) has been created to provide venture capital for new developments or companies of promise requiring financial support which is not normally available from conventional sources.

CED is neither a bank nor an investment company in a traditional sense; it is a builder of enterprises. In addition to supplying equity capital, it makes available to companies in which it actively participates the technical and administrative experience of its management, board of directors, and its advisers and friends in Canada and abroad.

But Doriot felt that effective international venture-capital investing could happen only if Europe had a fund as well. And he quickly set about to get the regulatory approvals that would ARD to operate a fund in Europe, albeit at arm's length. On March 18, 1962, Doriot wrote to the Securities and Exchange Commission.

We represent American Research & Development Corporation ("ARD") a registered closed-end investment company of the management type exempted from certain requirements of Section 12(a) of the Investment Company Act of 1940 to permit its common stock to be held by other investment companies pursuant to that section (ICA Release #934). ARD believes that its activities could be profitably extended to the European Common Market under the proper auspices and that the resulting interchange of ideas would be beneficial to ARD's activities in this country and a small contribution to sound national policy. It has concluded that ARD cannot expand into Europe directly with any good hope of success because of the natural desire of Europeans to protect and control for themselves the benefits of important ideas, process, techniques, and inventions with which such a project would be involved. ARD has, however, found increased European interest in a company which would be basically European but draw to some extent upon United States capital and experience. Such a vehicle ("ERD") is presently proposed for investment by ARD which would be one of its promoters in addition to two large New York banks and a number of European banks.

It took two more years before Doriot's idea for a European venture-capital fund that would be patterned after ARD but have its own cultural framework and own set of investment guidelines—to reflect the European reality—came true. The following was the release that ARD put out to mark the occasion:

> American Research and Development Corporation, which has made a profitable business of helping new scientific and technical enterprises get started in the United States, is exporting its mode of operation to Europe.
>
> General Georges F. Doriot, president of ARD, announced today the formation of European Enterprises Development Company, a venture-capital company to be patterned after ARD.
>
> Four American participants—the Boston-based ARD, Continental International Finance Corporation (Chicago), Lehman Brothers (New York), and Morgan Guaranty International Finance Corporation (New York)—each are investing the equivalent of $250,000 in the new company; sixteen European banks and other financial institutions are providing a total of $1,500,000. The total original capital, denominated in Luxembourg francs, is equal to $2,500,000.
>
> General Doriot, who is chairman and president of the European company, said:
>
> Together with ARD and CED (Canadian Enterprise Development Corporation Limited), it is planning to be of constructive help to companies on either side of the Atlantic who wish to develop their activities across the ocean.
>
> EED will interest itself in creating new companies and developing small or medium-size companies in Europe based on European or North American ideas and technology. EED will also interest itself in nations outside of Europe.

From the very beginning Doriot recognized the shortcomings of venture capital outside the United States. There were no real models of success. There weren't the capital markets that supported the needs of an entrepreneurial economy. Large industrial corporations controlled the economy and certainly weren't willing to give up their hegemony to raw start-ups, many operated by corporate refugees, or, as some described it, corporate castoffs.

The laws themselves were not favorable to entrepreneurial business formation. Even now, for example, Germany—one of the more advanced European entrepreneurial cultures—has laws on its books that impede small businesses from starting up. One such law requires all crafts businesses ranging from hairdressing to interior design to be headed by a Meister, a qualification that requires even the most experienced craftsworkers to take on years of additional training and costs over $50,000 in additional fees. Under the Meisterbrief restrictions, which are supported by the country's craft guilds and the larger corporations, competition is kept low and costs are pushed up. Indeed, a survey in 2002 estimates that the Meisterbrief restrictions have prevented the formation of as many as 500,000 businesses over the last decade.

Doriot saw such laws in evidence all across Europe. And while he hoped that many of these would in time be eased, he focused on areas in manufacturing and technology that were somewhat beyond the reach of their restrictions. He also hoped that the strengths and the reputation of EED's partners would offset some of the existing reluctance to do business with entrepreneurs and entrepreneurial start-ups.

But Doriot's optimism was not warranted. EED portfolio companies had to turn to traditional financing for their growth development and expansion since there was no initial public offering market for young companies. And when they ran into trouble they were treated not much differently than the way lenders treated more established borrowers. The start-ups were refinanced at newer, more onerous terms. They were asked to offer more collateral to cover the increased risks. Lenders then placed their own on the start-ups' boards of directors to manage the debt.

"We ended up with too many bankers," says Arnaud de Vitry, HBS Class of '53 and a director of EED. And when there was an entrepreneurial crisis, bankers behaved like bankers, not like venture capitalists. Moreover, the traditional European corporation did not feel comfortable doing business with start-up companies, effectively shutting them out of key business areas.

ARD meanwhile continued to prosper. Its investment in Digital Equipment Corporation was an enormous success, one of the most successful investments in the history of venture capital in a company that grew traditionally, without the aid of an inflated stock market.

In 1957, two scientists affiliated with MIT, Kenneth Olsen and Harlan Anderson approached ARD with the idea of designing and selling a scientific computer. While Doriot was completely taken by the idea and committed to invest, he worried that the idea of investing in a start-up with development-stage technology and no real product would convey the wrong ideas to his shareholders and investors. So the ARD annual report for 1957, while acknowledging the investment in Digital Equipment Corporation, obfuscates the goals of DEC. It says that "DEC manufactures and sells transistorized digital 'building block' units, improved versions of research, development, and testing devices." What DEC was building was a machine that would completely change the face of computing. And because there was very little to go on—no industry data, no competitive history, no market data—Doriot's investment truly was a shot in the dark.

But Doriot wasn't speculating. DEC's technology had the right pedigree. It came out of MIT, which at that time was the premier engineering institution in the U.S., if not the world. In the first years of its existence, nearly three out of four of ARD's technology investments had their origins at MIT. He also was counting on Olsen's vision, a vision that he grew to respect even more with time.

Olsen, now 77, says that he became convinced of the need for real-time computing after the war. He recalls pilots being frustrated that radar systems could track and plot the directions of planes but couldn't adequately calculate trajectories and intercepts. He also remembers how physically cumbersome such machines were. While canoeing in the Arctic, he encountered a bank of giant computers that NORAD then used to track planes and missiles. "They were very one-dimensional. They didn't seem to have any other purpose," he explains.

Olsen was convinced that real-time computing was necessary. And although he couldn't cite chapter and verse on the potential market, he was confident that the needs would emerge as the machines became available. He was emphatic enough in his vision to have convinced Doriot.

DEC's PDP (for Personal Data Processor) was by all computing standards a radical product. It changed the face of computing. But Olsen didn't want to merely dangle the promise in front of his investors. He went out of his way to create a design that non-technical investors would be comfortable with.

For his part, Doriot played the hands-off investor. He helped Olsen, Anderson and Olsen's brother find an abandoned mill space in Maynard and worked hard at keeping them focused on the technology tasks. He also made sure that the milestones DEC achieved were adequately communicated to investors and potential customers.

What role could Doriot and ARD have played in the growth and development of DEC?

"The role of mentor and champion," says Olsen. By today's standards, the amount of money—$70,000—was small. But Olsen and Doriot put together a board that was a model of its time. It was a board that was vested in technology and technology change and understood the unpredictability of bringing about that change. And unlike many of the directors that populated the Internet bubbles nearly a half-century later, these directors took their work seriously. MIT Professor Ed Morse recalls that one director resigned at the time of DEC's initial public offering because he felt that the financial results in the memorandum would mislead investors into believing that such results could be routinely replicated. The director felt that the company should specifically state that the numbers in question were unusual and should not be used as investment indicators.

The concern was legitimate. Investing in early-stage companies especially in technology—companies that had little track record and no fully defined product—was no sure thing. And Doriot and his board were concerned that disappointed investors would not only hurt DEC, but the entire universe of early-stage technology companies.

Doriot was first and foremost a champion of his companies. In the 1980s when DEC had become a mature technology company and was going through some missteps, Doriot continued to support the company. One of the snipers repeatedly attacking the company was *The Boston Globe*. Finally, when a *Globe* article written by reporter Ron Rosenberg criticized the company without failing to acknowledge its role as a pioneering Route 128 company, Doriot felt compelled to compose a response.

The letter was never sent but it exemplifies the role of champion that Doriot typically played on behalf of his portfolio companies.

To: Mr. Ronald Rosenberg
Globe Staff

Sir:
I have read your article in the Boston Globe dated 11 August 1982. It is headed: "Growth Rate Slow at Digital Equipment Corporation." I assume that you are appreciative of what Digital Equipment Corporation has done in its 25 years of existence. Of course, you know that under the leadership of Mr. Kenneth Olsen, the President, the Company started with a capital of $70,000 in a few rooms in an old mill in Maynard, Massachusetts. You know that today it employs over (?) [sic] hard working people. Do you understand what it has done for the town of Maynard? (Just to take one example.)

You know how politicians get credit for the development of so-called high technology in Massachusetts. You must know it because your newspaper gives them credit and writes long articles about them.

In this difficult economic period, when people are troubled, lose faith, do not have many things or people to admire, Mr. Rosenberg, could you not write an article which gives credit to a hard job well done, which gives hope, which gives praise, which gives, positively, the results of the wonderful people who work at Digital Equipment Corporation? Could you not show them some appreciation? Show faith in their work, their product, their company?

Do you understand my reaction to your uninteresting article? Do you understand what I am talking about? Or should I be reminded of vultures that thrive on blood, accidents, death, and troubles? If Digital Equipment Corporation had done poorly instead of exceptionally well in this difficult period, your task would have been so much easier and enjoyable. You could have written a long article about the troubles of the Company. Of course with much glee. You could have underlined your first sentence—"as expected." Newspapers have such great foresight particularly on subjects they have no knowledge of, and, of course, for which they carry no responsibility. You have a happy life but not very constructive.

Mr. Rosenberg, I have never written to a newspaper before. If it concerned me I would not care, but it concerns thousands of People for whom I feel friendship, respect, and admiration: the people of Digital Equipment Corporation. Mr. Rosenberg, be appreciative of people's work. It will help them and may help your conscience. I am certain that you mean well but you may be hampered by the demands of your profession—also by the people you work for.

Someday, why don't you try to get a job at Digital Equipment Corporation, and enjoy a constructive life? You might be surprised at the satisfaction one has participating in the building of useful products. Try it and then see whether you enjoy and appreciate what outsiders write about your work, your colleagues, and your products.

In the U.S., ARD was constantly championing the cause of its portfolio companies. It provided visibility to them by organizing technology fairs at its annual meetings, a portent of the future COMDEX. At the old John Hancock building where the ARD annual meeting was held, the portfolio companies presented themselves before ARD shareholders, a legion of securities analysts, potential corporate buyers and investors and partners. For young portfolio companies, these were pivotal events. It not only gave them exposure, but it also created vital connections with Wall Street and with corporate America.

In contemporary venture-capital practice, it is more than common to charge investors high management fees. The dollar amounts have become extraordinary as funds manage more and more money. Indeed, there are those who maintain that the high management fees charged by venture-capital funds are almost a disincentive to creativity and to company building. The rewards, at least in the present, seem to be geared more toward liquidity and quick exits rather than company building and value creation.

Doriot certainly had no such illusions. In spite of the stock market's cyclical aberrations and spikes, he was sure that companies needed to go public on established performance. That didn't mean that companies had to go public only when they were mature; technology created a different paradigm. But he had no desire to take companies public prematurely, have them falter and jeopardize the entire technology sector.

Such convictions, however, meant that ARD lived hand to mouth and ARD professionals enjoyed none of the lifestyle that modern venture capitalists with lesser success and far fewer notches on their belt have grown to expect and enjoy. Charles Waite, who was a student of Doriot and went on to work for him at ARD, says he left the firm because the compensation was totally disproportionate to the work that was demanded and the productivity generated.

The restrictions posed by the Investment Company Act on fund compensation practices meant that Doriot could never generate enough capital to adequately compensate his professionals. And while he may have shielded such problems with the grand vision of building a new economy and a new culture, he worried that the structure inhibited ARD and prevented him from attracting top talent. In the late 1960s he articulated some of these worries and ideas in a "management note":

- To run ARD, one needs ideals and skills.

- All the skills required need not be in the possession of the man, but he must understand them, secure them, stimulate them.

- There must be great harmony between ideals and skills.

Whether we like it or not, we must realize that most people did not think that ARD had any future. Then suddenly we became fashionable and everybody went in venture capital. We were never competitive from a compensation viewpoint. We have a hard time getting the type of men we should have and want. At first they could have options if they worked for an affiliate. They could have better income with normal companies, better compensation if they were in investment banking. Later on when venture capital became of age they could form partnerships (done long before by Rockefellers, Whitneys, etc.) For a long time working for ARD did not seem interesting: Long hours, much traveling, no security, questionable future, low salaries. Our salaries had to be low because we had no income, and it was felt that we should pay dividends. Now we can pay good salaries and other benefits, but we must find ways to get very much more income from our investments. Our present income is due to cash and high interest rates. Cash is coming down as we invest, and interest rates are also coming down. Paying salaries out of capital gains means operating at a loss which, rightly or wrongly, I do not like to do.

For Doriot, venture capital was a missionary activity. And he searched far and wide for those who believed in the mission. As ARD expanded its sphere of activity from the Massachusetts region, he saw the need to find those who could promote venture capital and help in the deal flow. In 1969, he recruited Dan Holland, then a junior banker in Chicago as his Midwest lookout. It wasn't long before Holland moved to Massachusetts.

What was it like working for Doriot?

Says Holland:

The General had an interesting way of using a lot of people who were students. ARD had two correspondents, one in Houston and one in Los Angeles. The guy in Houston worked at a commercial bank. General Doriot then came to the First National Bank of Chicago where I was working and the president of the bank had been a student of the General's. Doriot said he would like someone in the Midwest to be a correspondent for ARD, someone who would work for nothing in his spare time, nights and weekends, and be its representative in the Midwest. I got elected to do that.

In those days venture capitalists had to work hard to unearth investment opportunities. There wasn't a network. People didn't know venture capital existed. We spent a lot of time marketing, It was difficult to find entrepreneurs flowing into venture firms with ideas that they wanted backing. We spent a lot of time marketing, selling, trying to convince people that we were a good source of money. Send us all your ideas. We will sift through and invest in some of them. We worked hard at getting a continual flow of ideas coming through and that was basically what they asked me to do in the Midwest.

One day the General came to Chicago and said he would like to meet with me. "We are very unhappy with having you here in the Midwest working for us," he said jokingly. "We think you should come back to Boston and work with us." I went home to talk to my wife and we decided it would be a big risk but we'd do it. Leaving the bank was no risk at all. We moved back to Boston with our four kids. The General didn't know I had four children. He had no children. Very few people within ARD had children. John Shane and Bill Congleton had two each.

Doriot knew that I had worked at MIT and had good contacts and was very interested in getting into the guts of MIT. I brought out whatever investments I had been involved in three years as industrial liaison officer at MIT prior to working for the bank.

I was the first person to join who was not a former student of his. I had opportunity to take his course when I was at the Harvard Business School in 1952 and he did a big selling job. You had to attend a meeting in which he outlined his philosophy of teaching and manufacturing and he talked a lot about hard work and dedication and I said "Yes, I heard all these before," and he also made it clear that you had to totally dedicate yourself to his course. I was getting married that September and I got a new bride coming on board, I wasn't going to totally dedicate myself to anybody's course. So I didn't take his course but when I joined ARD he said, "Well, you weren't a student of mine like Shane, Morgan, Congleton." And he said while there was a big void in my background, it was probably one that I could make up by attending class with him every Saturday. So I was expected to come in and spend three hours learning. Doriot loved working Saturdays. Saturday had been a standard workday in ARD for years by that time. If a special project came up the General loved to have everybody meet on Saturday to discuss it. There was no training program, just come in and go to work. He obviously had people in there who were very dedicated to him and that was important to him.

By that time ARD was trading on the New York Stock Exchange and had 11,000 stockholders. At their annual meeting every year in Boston all the ARD portfolio companies came to exhibit. It was the forerunner to contemporary trade shows. We would have 25 to 30 companies all with their company exhibits and Wall Street and everybody looking to see what was going to be the new outlook of ARD and the exhibiting companies. It was one of the biggest shows in New England at the time. They would have a big dinner for all the CEOs of the companies, a major function. That's how you learned the business; you learned from other people in it. In those days you didn't have the Internet. You really had to work to get investment deals coming through.

The General was clearly the person in charge, magnificent at pulling together all kinds of ideas and people always thinking, questioning and dreaming that ARD should have some major project. We had a project trying to build a tunnel under the English Channel, in those days you always had to have some big dream. DEC was not a dream at that point—it was a successful venture.

The General had totally dedicated people working with him, his secretary Pat Clark and Dorothy Rowe. It was hard to figure out how ARD would run. What the success formula was it wasn't apparent, but it was very clear that he was people oriented. He was good and a hero to the people he backed. He was always looking for that spark of genius and entrepreneurial spirit. He was very insistent on meeting that person and that was his form of success.

At ARD, generally everybody was out looking for their own deals. We had a personal advocacy approach. You were expected to work deals through yourselves, yet get help from other people when you needed it. You had to have a backup, spend a lot of time understanding the people involved and their motivation and the market and technology. Doriot insisted on deep immersion in any investment before you made it. In those days you could do that. You could take several months to look at an investment and the final OK had to come from the board of directors. You looked at the board of directors that he had assembled masterfully. It was a very impressive board. He handpicked each of those people probably more so than he picked the people who worked for him.

Most of the successful companies at ARD came out of MIT. You tried to prove the technology where you could and understand as well as you could. The first company ARD invested in was a shrimp farm and that almost felled ARD. The next investments were in engineering and high tech and they all came out of MIT. DEC came out of MIT, to a degree. Ken Olsen was working at MIT's Lincoln Laboratory when he did it. To look at ARD, it was basically started by MIT. The first three advisers were MIT professors. There were four or five college endowments involved when the fund raised money and MIT was one. ARD was very heavily MIT oriented in the early years.

For Doriot most of the excitement was in new technologies. He would get intrigued with anything that was new and revolutionary. He called us up one day to come in on a Saturday because there was a guy from Michigan who came in and said he had a breakthrough in nuclear fusion. "We can't tell anybody about what we have but we owe the banks and this whole breakthrough might be lost," the scientist said. The General had called someone on the Atomic Energy Commission and his contact said he couldn't tell Doriot anything about it but the whole team at the commission got together the other day to discuss it. I was told to go out and take care of the bank and it turned out they had a possible breakthrough in nuclear fusion. These were the kind of people that intrigued him.

In the early days, the rewards came from the General dealing out positions in the portfolio companies. ARD staff members would become directors of the portfolio companies and in some cases get stock options. ARD in the early years financed itself by charging consultant fees. There was no management fee. It was a public-owned company and we weren't charging fees to manage assets. Consulting by the General and others paid the ARD salaries. Doriot wanted to show a profit so each of the companies had to pay a consultant fee when they received an ARD investment. The fee was justified on the basis that every time that CEO signed a check every month to pay ARD he would think about how he should be using us and staying in contact with us. The people were rewarded with small options in the company they were sitting on. And in DEC, among the people who were on the board there were people like Dorothy Rowe and Bill Congleton. At sometime Ken Olsen said: "I think there should be stock options for each of the directors too." So they each got options which became worth $30 (million) to $40 million down the road. Bill Elfers, who was the senior person at ARD at the time, but not on the board of DEC, didn't get stock options and more or less saw these three other people passing him by immensely in terms of wealth. That's when he left. By the time I joined ARD you could not have stock options in an investment-backed company. The General did not have any stock in DEC.

The dominant theme at ARD? It was a combination of good people that were always first, and the technology. You did everything you could in terms of talking to people who knew about the technology, using all the General's contacts in various industries. Here's the concept, what do you think of it? For the fusion thing, for example, the General called the Atomic Energy Commission and in the meantime we tried to check out if this fusion idea could work while Dan was out trying to tell the bankers why they shouldn't pull their notes. You could not get a definitive "yes this will work" but you backed people who would hopefully make it work. We did win on that and backed some deals that wouldn't. We backed a magazine for industrial research dedicated to industrial labs, research labs and industry. The reason the General backed that—before I got here but I ended up going on the board of the company—was because with all the research labs all over the world subscribing to this and all the new ideas we would find some investment opportunity.

During ARD's time there was a heavy emphasis on finding great entrepreneurs. The characteristics you run down are intelligence, dedication, energy, vision, but mostly it's like perfume—you can't really describe it, but when you smell it you know it's good. You have to spend a lot of time with somebody and getting to know them and getting inside their head and making sure that you have a good feeling that they have entrepreneurial capabilities. You spend a lot of time with them in different settings: sales calls, labs, workplace, dinner with the wife, mostly just spending a lot of time and getting a feeling for how they approach and solve problems.

How did we distinguish the good from the bad? The good entrepreneurs had to be hard working, have vision, good experience dedication. They had to have the ability to find good people, intelligent. There is no easy logarithm that you can plug in a bunch of variables and boom and that comes out to 95-100 he's good, or 85, below that he's not. There was no index. The entrepreneur had to meet everybody in ARD. You could spend more time then. The last hurdle they had to go through was to make a presentation to the ARD board of directors and that board had some of the top industrial and financial people in the nation on it. The board had no prior knowledge of what they were going to be presented with. The General was very clear; he orchestrated his board beautifully.

They came in and were presented with the investments to approve and they were given material and they had to listen to this poor entrepreneur get up there and make this bid. They usually said yes. I had one turned down by the board. It was a blood plasma replacement basically using saline water as a plasma substitute. They were not impressed and the guy didn't make a good presentation. They were saying: "This is water!" It got shot down. The entrepreneur had to go through a lot of hoops, but you usually did fall in love with them.

There is no similarity between today and what ARD was. Today's venture-capital industry is so much bigger. More money involved and opportunities for people to seek investors so the entrepreneurial times have changed. It was more approachable in the early days. There were very few buyers. We used to have to go out and promote ourselves. Now, venture capital is much more understood. There was a real fear of losing money. Part of the reason was there was very little money to work with. The other part was that deep association of attachment that you developed for the investment that caused you to put a tremendous amount of effort in one deal. Oftentimes you were the only investor and you were intensely involved. You spent more time trying to keep deals from going bad. You didn't spend a lot of times enhancing those deals that were going good. You were spending 50% of your time trying to save two bad deals in which you might save a half million, instead of 50% of your time on a deal that was increasing in value from $5 million to $50 million. It turns out there was probably little you could do on the upside for these companies. They were doing it themselves. You were probably better off staying out of them so you spent a lot of time working on the difficult ones. There wasn't any syndication. It was clubby in those days with two or three firms that always worked together, there were so few firms. There was no defined sectors in ARD. We would invest in any-thing— technology, magazines, and electric motor manufacturing, sea technologies, an egg farm in Minnesota. There was no specialization. Nor did we try to predict. We always relied on the entrepreneurs. They were the ones who had to predict.

MIT Professor Ed Morse remembers the time he set up a meeting with General Doriot. Morse had been looking at the common themes in ARD's investments and wanted to discuss some of them. "I figured that understanding what ARD was looking for in its investments and how it invested would help entrepreneurs approach funding more efficiently," he says. Doriot was extremely evasive, recalls Morse. There wasn't a methodology to the strategy, Doriot insisted. Besides, said the General, the criteria were proprietary and he didn't want to give them away.

Doriot may have been putting Morse on but he wasn't far from the truth. There wasn't a blueprint for investing. And while all of the professionals at ARD had a love for technology and for entrepreneurship, there simply wasn't the rush to technical and statistical analysis that characterizes much of venture-capital investing today.

Doriot's venture investing was people first. He firmly believed that an entrepreneur with the right motivation and the right set of skills was the most important element in any successful investment. He was not averse to the business idea or the business plan, but he felt that the right entrepreneur, with the correct amount of support, was always the key element in any decision.

Said Doriot:

In evaluating a new situation, the quality of the investigation is far more important than quantity. In many cases, the venture investor is studying new products for applications where previous business or technological history is relatively inadequate. For example, qualitative marketing research which seeks out specific people with pertinent knowledge and experience is more important in this type of study than consumer panels or substantive field tests.

The principal judgment fact as required is an evaluation of the management of the company under consideration. It always must be recognized that a venture can be expected to demonstrate at the outset only some of the important elements for success, rather than present a neat, tidy package which can be evaluated solely by financial yardsticks.

Since evaluating the management is considered the most important analysis factor, American Research has charted the characteristics of successful young managers. Some of these follow: The top management must have technical creative competence. The entrepreneur and his top associates must have a drive for recognition or monetary reward.

Hard work is a prerequisite for the success of any one of these managers supplemented by a balanced personal life. Creative capital can always supply the funds for such a venture, but basically, men are required for what is always a man's work.

In conducting an investigation of a new venture, American Research relies on the capabilities of its own staff, its 15 years of operating experience, and its many and wide contacts in all fields. A principal source of projects and evaluation assistance is the current family of affiliates in which there exists a diversity of technical talent probably not matched by anyone other single corporation in this country. The staff maintains contact with investment bankers, commercial banks, auditing firms, universities, and research organizations. In addition, many of its 5,700 stockholders, both individuals and institutions, have been and continue to be a great source of help.

The 15-year record of American Research, even during a period of bull-market activity, compares favorably with the general market averages. The search, analysis, and cultivation of young companies can be financially rewarding to those who have the financial and managerial resources to pursue this capital objective.

Venture capital, in a formal organization like American Research, can prove its opportunity of success and reduce its chance of failure participating as an active partner in each project. There is always a critical job to be done, because small, new companies live in a dynamic atmosphere, replete with minor crises. There is a sales door to be opened, a credit line to be established, a new important employee to be found, or a business technique to be learned. The venture investor must always be on call to advise, to persuade, to dissuade, to encourage, but always help build. Then, venture capital becomes true creative capital—creating growth for the company and financial success for the investing organization.

Like other venture capitalists of his time, ARD would scrupulously vet every entrepreneur that came looking for money. Peter Crisp, HBS Class of '60, a student of General Doriot and later a venture capitalist with New York's Venrock Partners, talks of venture capitalists who would even visit with entrepreneurs' families to make sure that they fit the bill. Doriot also met the families and put trust in entrepreneurs and families who merited ARD's investment.

Of course, there wasn't much room for crystal balls or even for informed projections. Although technology companies were established in the marketplace and technology products were in demand, projections were flawed and misleading. When Max Palevsky, a West Coast entrepreneur, needed capital for his scientific computers, the famed Rand Corporation projected that there was little demand for such machines, certainly no more than two to three over the next decade. That same idea did get funded and the subsequent company, Scientific Data Systems was sold to Xerox for nearly $1 billion in 1969.

Perhaps aware of the problems of research projections, Doriot focused on his own due diligence. Each professional was asked to take responsibility for a potential investment and ask the questions that any potential investor would ask. What kind of customers would the product have? Has the management any experience with similar products? Would corporate customers have any interest? Were there similar products out there? Can the company generate sales and revenue in a reasonable period of time?

Ironically, even though ARD's charter required it to invest in companies with products and, possibly, sales, its biggest returns came from technology start-ups such as DEC and Teradyne.

Because much of the future of a technology couldn't be properly gauged, Doriot decided to focus on understanding the market for a product. And he used his vast network of students and business contacts to carry out the task. The General didn't seem to have much faith in consultants for help in understanding new products, simply because he felt they didn't have the incentives to understand new markets. They were better at solving problems.

Doriot saw the market for his entrepreneurial companies in global terms. He recognized the fact that the primary market for most products were in the U.S., but he also recognized the nascent development stage that many countries in Europe were in, and he encouraged many of his entrepreneurs to actively seek out customers across the Atlantic. DEC, for example, established its first connections in Europe as early as the 1960s.

Although U.S. industrial companies were already in global markets and many European and Japanese companies were trading with the U.S., Doriot may have been among the first venture capitalists to see the globe as a natural arena for venture capital and entrepreneurial companies. And he saw the existence of ARD and its foreign counterparts as a seamless whole.

> I have told you about the Canadian and the European companies. To some people that sounds like something ordinary. After all, one can go to a lawyer's office or to some State House, sign papers, put up money, and thereby a new company is formed. This, gentlemen, is not the case with CED and EED. Those two companies and ARD do have what I would call a material value, but way beyond that, they have a spiritual value, and that spiritual value I rate far above the material value one may place on them. It is my sincere belief that spiritual, moral constructive values have to be placed above anything else in life. Otherwise our physical existence has no meaning.

There are those who argue that Doriot was much too missionary in his approach to venture capital. He couldn't have delivered the needs of asset managers today. But Doriot, more than most venture capitalists today, recognized the fragile nature of technology start-ups and their lack of predictability. As a publicly traded company that had to regularly report on the condition of its investments, ARD had to disclose each of its investments but Doriot repeatedly pointed to some of the problems of such disclosure.

> Thinking of the valuation of the affiliates and remembering what I have said earlier, I might say that, leaving out the few very large companies in which ARD has an investment because of a sale to them of some

of our affiliates, I would suggest that our other affiliates, the ones that correspond to our normal type of investment, should not be judged on the basis of less than a full year's record.

For the management of a young company there is a choice to be made: When a young company becomes traded on a public market, the management learns about a rather new and interesting activity called financial analysis. We learn that financial analysts would like quarterly and, if possible, daily reporting of sales and profits. Those sales and profit figures are expected to show constant and even growth according to a mythical and movable ratio of some sort.

Any relatively new company, particularly a technical one, cannot be operated on such short time conception. Those companies are interested in taking constructive steps to maximize their growth—stability and profitability. Many of those steps, and expenditures, particularly engineering—new facilities, etc., are often an important part of the total volume of business of a small company. Those expenses, while planned and programmed, are bound to take place sometime during the year. Good accounting procedure calls for them to be absorbed when they take place. It does not seem good procedure to spread them out merely to please people who usually have no manufacturing experience or responsibility for the future of a company.

A speculator or certain type of what is called investor can get in and out of a company at will. Management of companies plan to stay with their company for a fairly long period. Therefore, having to make a choice between pleasing people with temporary interest vs. pleasing people with a long-term interest is an easy decision from my standpoint. I suggest that our companies be judged on the basis of at least a year's work. In our line of work, it is better to be industrially oriented than stock-market oriented.

INVESTMENT PIONEER

Scientific Risk-Taking Keeps Paying Off
for American Research & Development

DAVID A. LOEHWING

(Published in 1960 this articles predates the success of Digital Equipment Corporation, ARD's most successful investment.)

"The boom in equities of Small Business Investment Companies is due, in part, to the tax loss advantage they offer the high income set. That's not the case with us. We're not in the business of producing losses."

—General Georges Doriot, president,
American Research & Development

BOSTON — EARLY LAST MONTH, 350,000 shares of American Research & Development Corp. common were offered to the public at $24.70 each, thereby raising more than $8 million for further ventures in what company officials call "enlightened capitalism." Snapped up eagerly, the shares soon were selling for a dollar above the offering price. This reception was in sharp contrast to that given ARD equities when the company was launched 11 years; ago as the world's first publicly held investment concern specializing in furnishing venture capital to new companies, In 1946, brokers were willing to handle the

77

stock only on a "best efforts" basis and not until 1951 were all the shares sold. An official of Lehman Brothers, which headed this year's underwriting syndicate, says: "American Research now is considered a seasoned, quality issue."

This estimate is a fair measure of the distance ARD has traveled since Wall Street viewed it as a sort of freak philanthropic enterprise dreamed up in Boston by a strange assortment of Harvard professors and State Street financiers. There are other yardsticks. One is the rise of competition; in recent years, a dozen or more new concerns, including those financed in part by the government under the Small Business Investment Company Act, have followed the path pioneered by ARD. Another is its own growth. ARD's net worth, as of June 30, had risen from $3.4 million to an impressive $30.8 million.

The company, moreover, gained its success by investing in some of the most glamorous ventures on the U.S. corporate scene, firms which are exploring the frontiers of modern science and technology. It has substantial holdings, for example, in Tracerlab Incorporated, which specializes in nucleonics; Ionics Incorporated, which makes a membrane system for converting brackish or salt water into fresh; Itek Corporation, which makes data storage and retrieval systems; High Voltage Engineering Corporation," which is the nation's leading manufacturer of nuclear particle accelerators; Avien Incorporated, which makes missile checkout systems; Technical Studies Incorporated, which was set up to evaluate plans for a tunnel under the English Channel; and Geotechnical Corporation, which is involved in the infant science of detecting underground nuclear explosions.

Through investments like these, ARD has prospered to such an extent that it has made some distribution to stockholders in every year since 1954. In 1956, 1957 and 1958, it spun off part of its holdings in High Voltage Engineering Corporation, and last year it paid $1 in cash. Early this year the stock was split, 3-for-1, and at midyear a 31-cent payment was made on the new shares. Altogether, those who originally bought ARD shares at $25 have received dividends of cash and stock amounting to over $42 (at current market values), some of it tax-free. More importantly, the asset value of the shares has tripled, and the rate of growth is accelerating. Last year, on assets of $14.8 million on January 1, and an additional $3.7 million from sale of 100,000 shares in April, ARD rang up unrealized capital gains of $5.3 million. In the first six months of this year, despite a sluggish market, the company piled up additional appreciation of $7.7 million. As of June 30, its net asset value stood at nearly 10 times what it was when the venture was launched. Clearly, then, the story of this Back Bay *parvenu* merits a closer look.

Conceived by former Senator Ralph E. Flanders of Vermont, then president of the Boston Federal Reserve, and Merrill Griswold, chairman of the Massachusetts Investors Trust, ARD was designed to fill what he considered a chink in the nation's economic armor. High wartime taxes had dried up the sources of risk capital; wealthy individuals, who normally finance such ventures, were reluctant to do so because any profits would be siphoned off by the government. Flanders and Griswold felt that the nation's liquid wealth was being concentrated excessively in fiduciary hands. "The prosperity of America," the Senator declared, "depends on finding financial support for new ideas and developments which give promise of expanded production and employment and a higher standard of living. We cannot float along indefinitely on the enterprise and vision of preceding generations."

The Senator's sentiments were echoed by such men as Karl T. Compton, then president of Massachusetts Institute of Technology, and several professors of that school, who served as consultants to the newly-organized company. More to the point, it also received the enthusiastic support of some eminent financiers. Paul Clark, president of John Hancock Life Insurance Corporation; Lessing J. Rosenwald, former chairman of Sears, Roebuck; David Luke, president of West Virginia Pulp & Paper; and Thomas Lamont, late chairman of J.P. Morgan & Corporation, all subscribed to the first stock issue, and several still serve as directors.

Setting up a closed-end investment company to fulfill the need Mr. Griswold and Senator Flanders discerned, however, was not easy. "It never could have been done without the understanding and active cooperation of the Securities and Exchange Commission and the Treasury Department," recalls Mr. Griswold. "They have been magnificent, under both Democratic and Republican administrations." At one point, when the venture appeared to be stymied by a provision in the law barring it from being treated, for tax purposes, as an investment trust, Griswold appealed directly to Congress, which pushed through enabling legislation.

Nor were the early results of the experience overly encouraging. While the founders of ARD were interested in giving the national economy a lift, not in adding to their personal fortunes, they were well aware that the firm hardly could succeed unless it showed a good profit. Yet it was eight years before the company's original stockholders received their first dividend or witnessed more than a nominal growth in the value of their shares. Many grew discouraged and sold out (Barron's, June 10, 1957). However, as already noted, for those who kept faith, the venture has paid off rather handsomely.

Directors credit much of this achievement to Georges Doriot, a French-born professor of industrial management at Harvard Business School and World War II brigadier general, who became president of ARD in 1946 when Flanders went to the Senate, A gentle, soft-spoken man, he seems ill-suited to the title "General" except that he goes about investing American Research money with a sort of idealistic fervor, as though directing a crusade. The entire operation is carried on from a small office in Boston's John Hancock Building, manned by a half-dozen key people, all of whom appear fired with a comparable zeal. It is one of the few offices in Boston open for business on Saturdays.

Asked if he soon will be forced to enlarge the staff, now that the business is expanding, General Doriot smiles, "No, we will all just work later into the night." Operating expenses of the company run to less than 1% of net asset value, a ratio which Mr. Griswold calls "fantastically low for this kind of work."

While the ARD portfolio over which these people watch consists mostly of securities of science-oriented companies, it contains also stocks of some concerns which have set themselves more mundane tasks. These include National Equipment Rental Ltd., which leases machinery and other capital equipment to industry; The National Key Corporation, which makes key duplicating machines and jewelry; Zapata Off-Shore Corporation, which operates sea-going drilling rigs; Carlon Products Corporation, which manufactures plastic pipe and tubing; and the Lewis Welding & Engineering Corporation, which does welding and makes heavy machinery.

While many of the latter investments have been profitable, most of ARD's failures have arisen when it wandered away from scientific research. In the early years, for instance, the company made several sorties into the food business, which turned up little in the way of either nutrients or dividends. One was Apple Concentrates Incorporated, a company which sought unsuccessfully to market quick-frozen apple juice. A tuna fishing expedition in the South Seas, financed in conjunction with Rockefeller Associates, failed to locate tuna in commercial quantities. ARD also dropped $307,000 in a company formed to market deveined shrimp.

More recently, owing to the decline of investor interest in the petroleum industry, the market value of ARD's 20,000 shares of Zapata Off-Shore Company has dropped to $100,000, from the $190,000 paid for them, even though the company last year climbed out of the red. A $1.6 million stake in Midwestern Instruments Incorporated, which makes magnetic tape-recording equipment, now is valued at $664,404. Finally, ARD directors now list $60,000 securities of a firm called Jet-Heet Incorporated, for which they paid $277,643.

These disappointments, however, fade into insignificance when placed alongside ARD's numerous successes, Its 85,000 shares of Cameo Incorporated, to cite one instance, cost $282,000 when that affiliate was developing pumping equipment for oil and gas fields; now they are worth $913,750 in the over-the-counter market. A $400,000 investment in Cramer Controls Corporation, which makes electro-mechanical timing controls, has appreciated to more than five times that figure. Holdings of Tracerlab, Textron Electronics, National Key, Ling-Tempo Electronics and Raytheon all have more than doubled in price.

ARD has scored its greatest gains in Airborne Instruments Laboratory, Ionics Incorporated, and High Voltage Engineering. An investment of $214,677 in Airborne Instruments, since absorbed by Cutler-Hammer, now is worth some $2.5 million. Similarly, in financing the formation of Ionics, ARD put up $402,843 in return for 216,929 shares of common stock, or a 40% interest in the company, Those shares now are quoted at about $6.5 million. Best of all, the funds $200,000 stake in High Voltage Engineering appreciated to $13.3 million (including, at their current price, the 62,342 shares spun off as ARD dividends in recent years).

In the early years, ARD was plagued by the general impression that it was a philanthropic organization. One magazine of vast circulation, indeed, published an article on the company entitled "If You Need $100,000 Or So —," indicating that anyone with an idea for giving the economy a lift need only apply in order to receive financing.

Nothing could be further from the truth. While General Doriot and his staff tend to favor ventures which they think will make a real contribution to the economy, their first consideration in selecting an investment is whether it will be profitable. Not a cent is ever is handed over to an affiliated company without a realistic appraisal of its money-making potential.

Over the years, executives of the firm have given serious study to exactly 3,284 projects; ARD has put money into 62. Before it extends aid in a company, every facet of the latter's operation is investigated thoroughly. When finally satisfied that the would-be affiliate is worthy of its interest, moreover ARD officials insist on a fair share of potential profits in return for the risk the company assumes.

A few recently consummated deals serve to illustrate the point. Adage Incorporated, a Cambridge, Mass., manufacturer of automation equipment, needed money for working capital and new machinery. ARD lent the firm $296,250 on a 6% note, due in 1967, and took an option to purchase 15,000 shares of Adage common stock. A loan of $300,000 was granted to Geotechnical Corporation on tile same terms, in return for options on 1,091 shares of common. Medical and Science Communications Development Corporation, which publishes a weekly newspaper for doctors, gave options on 125,000 shares in return for a $125,000 loan, due next year. Cordis Corporation, a manufacturer of medical instruments got $225,000 for expansion purposes, half of which must be repaid, with interest at 6½% by 1967; for the other half ARD took 900 shares of common, or a 30% interest in the company.

As a rule, ARD seeks out the companies in which it invests its money, rather than waiting for opportunity to knock on the door. In the case of Adage Incorporated, for example, ARD officials had heard about the company and became intrigued by the possibilities in its line of analog-to-digital conversion equipment for automatic process control. "We went to them and asked if there was anything we could do to help them get better established," recounts General Doriot. "At the time they seemed to have no problems, but later, when they needed additional working capital, they came to us."

Geotechnical Corporation, on the other hand, was what the General calls "an old friend of the family." Dr. William Heroy, its president, is one of the nation's foremost geologists and former head for Sinclair Oil. General Doriot asked him to serve on the board of directors of Diamond Oil Well Drilling Company ("I spend a lot of my time getting outstanding men to become directors of affiliates. It always pays off.) Dr. Heroy later acquired his own company, and when he needed expansion capital, he turned to ARD. The firm makes seismographs and other devices for detecting earthquakes and underground explosions and has government contracts to try to devise methods to keep the Russians from cheating if a pact halting nuclear testing ever is signed.

The Medical and Science Communications Development Corporation is a pure Doriot creation. "I have felt for a long time that we should be doing something in both the communications and health fields," the General says. "This is a way to kill two birds with one stone." The firm began publication in March of the *Medical Tribune*, a weekly newspaper for doctors.

The investment in Cordis Corporation also is the result of General Doriot's interest in medical matters. The company, headed by Dr. William Murphy, Jr., son of a Nobel Prize winner in medicine, makes advanced research and therapeutic equipment. One device, engineered by the company, is expected to become indispensable in hospitals for the treatment of heart ailments. Known as a Cardiac Programmer, it "listens" to the patient's heartbeat and activates, with exactly the same rhythm, a tiny pump which amounts to an auxiliary heart; this relieves the natural organ of the duty of working overtime to dissolve a blood clot. The company also makes and distributes equipment devised by other doctors and researchers. One such device is used in laboratories to record the heart beats of three-day-old chickens; it was developed in cooperation with a researcher at the University of Miami School of Medicine. Cordis applied to ARD when it needed funds for expansion because a partner, John Sterner, is a former official of Baird Atomics, an early ARD affiliate. "It was only natural for him to come to us, because he knows how we operate," says General Doriot, with pride.

While ARD, as noted, puts its money into relatively few projects, anyone can get a hearing—and, in many cases, real assistance. General Doriot believes that he should do what he can for any entrepreneur seeking his aid. Hence, American Research headquarters in Boston constantly is besieged by would-be industrialists, some lugging inventions, others carrying supposedly money-making schemes in their heads. (After the aforementioned magazine article, the company received an average of 70 letters a day.) Many of the ideas have real merit, and even though they fail to meet ARD's investment standards, the applicants are given sound advice on how to carry them out.

Indeed, some years ago General Doriot set up an affiliate, the Product Development Corporation, to extend a helping hand to inventors. It consisted of one man, an inveterate tinkerer named John Rockett, who sought markets for minor inventions on a fee basis—the fees to be paid by the companies buying them. ARD invested $10,000 in this venture, and eventually sold it for $14,000.

After investing in an affiliate, ARD doesn't stop there. General Doriot and other officials promptly put on their other hats as executives of American Research Management Corporation, a wholly-owned subsidiary, which provides consulting services to portfolio concerns. They help out with marketing and technical problems, straighten out legal tangles, and when the company is ready to go public (a goal sought for every affiliate), advise on stock-flotation procedures. "Our biggest hurdle usually is convincing them they need our help," says General Doriot. "The heads of these small companies, especially if they are scientists with no business experience, think they know all there is to know about setting up a company. But we don't hold that against them. If they weren't self-confident, they would be holding safe jobs somewhere and wouldn't be going into business for themselves in the first place."

ARD sometimes goes to great lengths to help its affiliates. Miss Dorothy Rowe, the treasurer, fulfills that function also for one portfolio firm not yet big enough to afford its own treasurer. When Ionics Incorporated, was formed, it encountered sales resistance because the government and officials of other companies thought it lacked "standing." When newspapers reported that Merrill Griswold (Chairman of the Board, Massachusetts Investors trust) had joined the board of directors, it began to win contracts. The president of another affiliate reported that he would not be able to attend to his duties for ten days because his wife had gone to the hospital to have a baby, and he had to do the housework. Overruling all wifely objections, he promptly dispatched the Doriot family maid to the scene. (His only regret is that she never came back.)

While American Research subsists on, and normally reports a small operating profit from interest and dividends from its affiliates, the company is interested primarily in capital gains. Hence, it usually retains its interest in each small company until the latter's equities can be offered to the public and a good market established. Then, General Doriot is faced with the same dilemma as any other successful investor—whether to hold or sell. The ARD board resolves the problem, with as much emphasis on a company's long-range technical capabilities as on current market quotations.

Looking at past decisions with the benefit of hindsight, some ARD stockholders might be inclined to quarrel with this viewpoint. Some high-flying glamour stocks in ARD's portfolio, such as Cutler-Hammer, Ionics, Itek, Raytheon and Tracerlab, have sold off sharply in the general market retreat of the past few months. On those five stocks alone, ARD's asset value has declined by nearly $2.5 million since its last report, June 30.

General Doriot insists, nevertheless, that the high price-earnings of those companies are based on solid technological achievement and that, barring a general market collapse, stocks eventually will regain the lost ground.

In any case, he is willing to stack ARD's performance, past or future, against that of any of the new venture-capital companies formed under the Small Business Investment Company Act of 1959. General Doriot, faithful to the concept that ARD was to light the way for other concerns entering the same field, says he welcomes the SBICs.

He describes himself as bemused, however, at seeing their equities selling at generous premiums, while ARD common is listed at a slight discount from reported asset value. He points out that while it will be some time before the investments of these new companies begin to pay off, ARD has been posting solid capital gains for eight years. "We pioneered this business and have 14 years of experience under our belts," he says. "Furthermore, we acquired it without any help from the government."

For the future, ARD plans to enlarge its scope. The $8 million raised via the recent stock issue will enable the company, in the words of General Doriot, "to attain a better balance between investments in new companies and existing ones." Much of the new money will be invested in established concerns. At the same time, the General has no intention of abandoning the original plan—to provide a source of capital for new enterprises. "The larger we are, the more creative we can be," he says. But then he adds: "I don't agree with the politicians that you should set a rate of growth. A healthy body will grow, regardless of norms. My job is to keep the body healthy."

AMERICAN RESEARCH & DEVELOPMENT CORP.

INVESTING IN THE ENTREPRENEURIAL COMPANY

General Doriot's remarks in connection with ARD Annual Report 15 July 1967

WHEN CONSIDERING AND THINKING about ARD's goals as stated in the ARD report, it must be apparent to stockholders that the type of work carried on in a venture-capital company such as ARD is quite different from the work of most other organizations.

Manufacturing companies are engaged in starting or launching new products. So is ARD. But there are many differences: ARD does not manage, does not control. It can help and advise, but it can seldom direct. ARD's advice can only be given to independent operators who are themselves stockholders of their own companies and who have other stockholders. There are usually commercial banks involved whose views must be considered and sometimes followed. Their views, which may or may not coincide with those of the management and of other stockholders, must be reconciled. The fact that ARD may be "deemed to control" by the SEC is often nothing but an illusion. It is easier to talk about control than to use it effectively or even have it available. In the case of ARD's portfolio companies, at least when they are very small, one product and more or less one man are the "whole." They are the company. If the man or the product is not effective and competitive, the "whole" of the company is in jeopardy.

In a large company there are many products, many lines of products, and many men. Individual products or human mistakes can more easily be absorbed and repaired. A small company starts and launches a product using capital. Existing companies use pre-tax money. Existing companies launch a new product while producing and selling existing ones. They have personnel, experience, background, trade relationships, etc. Their momentum and reputation allow and permit freedom of action while the new company is a one-bet affair, based on hopes and usually no "total" experience. The experience of the manager is usually limited to one of the many management factors so necessary for success in our highly competitive world. Effective control of operations, together with the ability to forecast fairly accurately, is difficult in a small company, particularly a new one. In a new company started from nothing or from very little, "figures speak too late." One has to be very sensitive and then very resourceful. Lack of background and experience are keenly felt. ARD's work is quite dissimilar to the standard work of many large investment institutions. ARD assets, like those of all investment institutions, are composed of securities, be they common or preferred stocks, notes, or convertible debentures. Most often, however, ARD's portfolio consists of securities of new companies that ARD has helped create, or of small companies which ARD has participated in. Early in the life of the companies, their securities are not traded and have no quoted market. If the companies prosper, the securities later are traded, but in many cases ARD is not free to sell them. Often, the SEC deems ARD to be in control. To remove itself from a control position to the SEC, ARD would have to withdraw the help it gives to those companies usually through representation on the board of those companies and also to dispose of some of its securities, probably at a time when it would be detrimental both to the company and to ARD. Often ARD would like to lighten its interest in some of its portfolio companies, but it hesitates to do so for fear that it might hurt the company's credit and future by giving the impression that ARD does not think as well of the future of that company as it used to. ARD has sometimes been criticized for staying too long with certain of its investments, but, looking back, ARD's standing has benefited from the fact that it has stayed with companies through their growth problems and diseases. Be that as it may, ARD is not in the business of trading in and out of the portfolio companies.

Sometimes there are restrictions on ARD's freedom to dispose of some of its securities. These restrictions are due to business judgment, some others due to regulations, the method of valuation of ARD's assets leading to a figure known as net asset value has been made clear to stockholders. To repeat, when the securities are traded, ARD must use the market valuation. When securities held by ARD are not listed on a national exchange or traded on the OTC market, it is the duty of the ARD board to set a fair value. Deciding on fair value for unlisted securities is not an easy problem. It requires mature experience, judgment, knowledge, and understanding of the companies involved. As the companies get older, their securities are usually traded, and the responsibility for proper determination of "value" is taken over by what is called "the market." It has been and is said that the market is always right and that the market is the best judge of value: By law, ARD has to use the judgment of the market for its listed securities.

Stockholders, traders, brokers are all part of what is called "the market." It is interesting to notice the results of the knowledge and wisdom of "the market." It might be disturbing to a less imaginative person to learn from specialists on the floor of the New York Stock Exchange that at times a great many people purchase stock in companies without any knowledge as to the nature of the company's business.

THE ARD RECORD

The following table shows the net asset value and distributions to stockholders since the company was formed. Per-share figures have been adjusted for the 3-for-1 split effected in 1960 and the 4-for-1 split effected in 1969.

YEAR END	Paid in on Outstanding Shares	Net Asset Value TOTAL	Net Asset Value PER SHARE
1971	$19,110,611	$427,769,774	$69.67
1970	19,110,611	332,774,925	54.20
1969	19,110,611	555,085,232	90.40
1968	19,110,611	385,976,991	62.86
1967	19,110,611	349,203,745	56.87
1966	19,110,611	93,000,414	15.15
1965	19,110,611	47,901,992	7.80
1964	19,110,611	38,799,228	6.32
1963	19,110,611	34,770,550	5.66
1962	19,110,611	30,708,373	5.00
1961	19,110,611	37,049,620	6.03
1960	19,110,611	38,875,003	6.33
1959	11,107,446	23,459,278	4.95
1958	7,357,047	14,795,999	4.18
1957	7,357,047	9,822,319	2.77
1956	7,357,047	10,811,394	3.05
1955	7,482,022	12,365,866	3.43
1954	7,482,022	10,998,132	3.05

	Paid in on Outstanding Shares	Net Asset Value	Net Asset Value
YEAR END		TOTAL	PER SHARE
1953	$7,482,022	$8,548,652	$2.37
1952	7,482,022	8,639,643	2.40
1951	7,482,022	7,899,305	2.19
1950	5,153,042	5,353,053	2.17
1949	4,465,356	4,526,497	2.13
1948	3,435,983	3,442,111	2.14
1947	3,658,245	3,532,192	1.95
1946	3,408,342	3,374,721	2.01

ARD Annual Report

THE MILITARY MAN

THE QUARTERMASTER CORPS

Building a Future: World War II Quartermaster Corps

Marcia L. Lightbody

(From The Military Review)

VALUABLE INNOVATIONS in the integration, coordination and attitude of service to the soldier were developed just before and during World War II by the Quartermaster Corps Military Planning Division under Brigadier General Georges F. Doriot. The division's task was to prepare soldiers for war in all possible climates. However, the only inventory on hand was leftover World War I clothing and equipment.

At a symposium in 1941, Doriot described the status of the Army's equipment: "Many items, which had been developed as the result of field experience in the mud and rain of Northern France in 1917 and 1918, were modified in peacetime to be more suitable for the garrison life at Fort Benning, Georgia, or Fort Sam Houston, Texas. Even after the outbreak of the war, [many did not recognize] the importance of immediately improving existing equipment."[1]

Creative Planning

In 1942, Captain Russell Davis, Doriot's executive officer, stared in amazement at a tank parked in his Washington, D.C., office parking lot. Only Doriot could have had a tank delivered to the parking lot. Davis recalls Doriot's words: "We have been asked to develop clothing for men who are going to be fighting in a tank. [I]f we are going to do it, we are going to have to have a tank."[2]

In planning, Doriot had an astounding grasp of detail and a passion for soldiers' well-being that pervaded his speeches and correspondence.[3] His far-reaching thoughts encompassed human engineering before ergonomics had a name.[4] Before 1942 it was unheard of to measure the width of foot space in a tank to see how much area a man's shoes might use, or the size of hand controls to understand what gloves he could wear.

In 1929, Quartermaster General Lieutenant General Edmund Gregory had attended one of Doriot's Harvard Business School courses. In 1941, Gregory persuaded Doriot to come into the Army. Gregory knew that Doriot's unusual personality traits included an abiding interest in the country's welfare and a pioneer's zeal in exercise physiology.

Roadblocks to Planning

Roadblocks to early military planning efforts were major. Robert Bates, who entered the Quartermaster Corps in early 1941 as an expert in cold weather and mountaineering, reported three impediments:

- By regulation, new equipment could not be provided until old equipment was used.

- No item could be procured in quantity until the theater

commander had approved it—and overseas commanders would not approve what they had not seen.

- If a new item was designed, the designer faced an extreme shortage of critical materials; metals and rubber were reserved for higher-priority planes, weapons, and vehicles.[5]

Between World War I and World War II, under the National Defense Act of 1920, military planning was based on a defensive concept that visualized military operations occurring mainly near or within the borders of the Continental United States or in similar climatic areas. Because the large stocks of surplus World War I clothing had to be issued until exhausted, little pressure existed before 1941 to manufacture new items.

Therefore, it was not surprising that in early 1942 the Military Planning Division faced a series of materiel disasters. Tents fell apart in the Southwest Pacific after two or three weeks because the fire-resistant finish had no fungicide to protect it against mildew. Troops in Alaska, preparing for a possible Japanese invasion, were largely immobilized by trench foot caused by ill-fitting and inadequately constructed footwear. An entire load of food had to be dumped into the ocean because the cans had rusted.[6]

Compounding the problem were some military leaders' viewpoints that rations were already the best in existence. Early in the war, a high-ranking general told Doriot that all soldiers needed in the way of supplies were coffee, beans, and blankets. He ordered Doriot not to spend any money on food research or on clothing.[7] It was not until after Bataan had fallen and a statement was made at a high-level meeting that the troops could have held out longer if the food had been of superior quality that ration development was transferred to the Military Planning Division.

Organizing Planning

The Military Planning Division's efforts had two thrusts—to acquire the division's own experts and research information in a hurry, and to establish a quartermaster advisory board that would include civil and military leaders. Doriot recruited staff for the division by culling War Department lists of new recruits who had attended courses at the Harvard Business School. He sought experts in every field. For example, by recruiting leaders in U.S. mountaineering and Arctic exploration, he acquired expertise in equipment and clothing for outdoor survival, cold-weather travel, and Arctic climatology.

His questions to those who joined the division were "what ifs" of every environmental possibility. The queries came in terms of combat. For example, what would happen if the United States had to support the Russians pushed by Germany into the Urals? The mountaineers found themselves conducting studies that included Arctic and Asiatic port conditions, sea ice, temperatures, and precipitation.[8]

Other experts arrived who were authorities on jungle conditions, packaging, leather, mechanical engineering, textiles and clothing, plastics, stress physiology, and Near East geology. Doriot's questions to all were "what if" or "can we." The first body armor was developed because Doriot asked, "Can we develop a bullet-proof vest?"[9]

The Military Planning Division was based on close coordination between those doing technical planning and development and those crafting operational plans and requirements for end items. The effect was that experts made immediate decisions. An item request did not go to procurement unless it was accompanied by a list of approved people to produce it, a statement of funds availability and War Production Board approval.[10]

After Doriot set up the advisory board, he made sure that members monitored the work at their own plants or institutions. He also listened to them. For example, he could ask Walter Chrysler for help with an automotive problem, and a pressing concern would get high-level attention. Industry leaders, under the stimulus of war, were eager to contribute expertise and facilities to solving design and materiel problems. The many offers of assistance required expert evaluation, coordination, and facilities. In time, the causes of deteriorating textiles in the tropics would be understood because of an intense in-house division laboratory effort.[11]

A number of university laboratories also contributed to the development program. The Harvard Fatigue Laboratory researched clothing principles, the efficiency of proposed items, and nutrition and exercise.[12] The University of Indiana Department of Physiology conducted laboratory testing of clothing for hot climates. The Tanners' Council laboratory at the University of Cincinnati analyzed leather problems.

The Military Planning Division's Requirements Branch was a small group of talented mathematicians who worked up the numerical requirements to clothe, feed, and equip an eight-million-man army. The mathematicians worked under intense pressure, using manual adding machines. Often they were told at the last minute that war strategy had changed, and their work had to be scrapped or repeated.

Innovations and Savings

By developing substitutes, particularly new uses for plastics, the Military Planning Division achieved extraordinary savings in critical raw materials. For example, redesigning button shanks on overcoats to use plastic rather than tin saved 90 tons of tin. During 1942, using plastic in some shoes saved 4,000 tons of rubber. By mid-1942, using substitutes and eliminating metal where possible, the savings for chrome, nickel, stainless steel, and aluminum was in the hundreds and thousands of tons.[14] Changing specifications because of shortages was not easy, but key factors in success were engineers, industrial specialists, field tests, and laboratory opinions.[15]

Short-term and prolonged equipment tests were highly creative. Tests conducted at the Harvard Fatigue Laboratory before the war were the basis for new tests that would determine the various supply product's feasibility and suitability. In the winter of 1941-1942, subjects with attached heat sensors tested sleeping-bag designs. The tests revealed the kind of comparative information that quantitative records on skin temperatures could provide, which led the Army to set up its own climatic-test chamber.[16]

When the war began, the services competed intensely for the limited supply of raw wool to use to insulate clothing. Two members of the Military Planning Division ran an informal test at the U.S. Department of Agriculture's (U.S.D.A.'s) cold research center in Maryland. Fourteen subjects wore standard Army coats identical except for the linings. A specialist from the Bureau of Standards controlled the thermocouples and the readings for each garment.[17] The researchers learned that regardless of what material was used, a garment's insulation was related to its thickness, as long as its exterior was windproof. Later experience showed the informal test results were also correct for still air.[18]

By February 1942, the cold weather group had from 30 to 40 items nearly ready for testing, but there was still no realistic test facility. The group initiated the Alaskan Test Expedition and spent over a month testing clothing and equipment in moderate to extreme cold on the slopes of Mount McKinley. Each member of the group wrote an evaluation of the items and changes were incorporated into finished products.[19]

The division also pushed the development of dehydrated foods and achieved savings in packaging, shipping bulk, and pack space. The effort to improve rations was continuous, and the use of dehydrated foods eliminated weight from the soldier's pack. Chancellor of the University of California at Davis Emil M. Mrak later remarked, "Natick (the Natick Lab) and its predecessor in Chicago have done more for the advancement of food science than any other agency."[20] The cooperation of the division and the U.S.D.A. in revolutionizing special Army food and packaging was heartening to government observers.[21]

In the early part of the war the division became interested in more effective approaches to the problems of flavor and food acceptance. The studies were a beginning effort to understand a broad range of practical problems in acceptance.[22]

The idea of using field observers to study soldiers' use of new equipment began early in the war. These efforts became the first Army marketing surveys. Observers traveled into combat areas, then reported to the Military Planning Division on quantities of products needed and any redesign or attention required. The independent observers' reports were critical to getting changes incorporated and problems fixed early in product use.

Selling Soldiers' Needs

Doriot was relentless in pursuing what can only be called a full-time campaign of selling soldiers' needs within the Armed Forces and industry. He later remarked, "We were able to foresee many needs before we were told about them."[23]

Doriot had two allies who played critical roles from the start—Gregory (his former student) and Army Chief of Staff General George Marshall. Doriot later commended the depth of Marshall's concern for the soldier and his helpfulness in cutting procurement delays. At their first meeting, Marshall informed Doriot, who had brought a bag of sample shoes, that "your shoes only last 13 days in combat. . . . Do you have anything to say?" Doriot replied, "Oh, yes, sir, a great deal. [F]or four or five months we have been trying to get staff approval for this combat boot and [we] can't get it. We know that our present shoes are not good for combat; the shoe leather isn't good; I'm surprised they even get to the combat zone." Marshall asked, "What do you want?" Doriot replied, "I want approval for that combat boot. Industry does not want to make it but we must have it. The ASF [Army Service Forces] Headquarters is completely opposed to it." Marshall thoughtfully said, "[T]his is a citizens' Army; I want them well taken care of; I want to save their lives and if you have to spoil them, do it and from now on any time you have trouble you come to me. What do you wish from me today?"[24] Doriot asked for 300,000 pair of shoes for a production test.

As to quality control, which was at first a major problem, the division was able eventually to devise quality-control statistical techniques for production line sampling that reduced Manufacturing errors from 25 percent to 5 percent.[25] The integration of all components of the soldiers' clothing, equipment, and rations into a unified whole was a goal expressed in 1943. Doriot conceptualized the design of the soldiers' items of clothing "in relation to each other," not as a large number of unrelated items.[26] Today's soldier system is its counterpart.

The effort to promote the soldiers' needs was successful in creating appreciation for new items of clothing, equipment and food among the military and for continually upgrading existing items. At Marshall's request, general officers received orientation to the division before assuming a field command.[27] Doriot's interest was in the well-being of all military personnel, not the Army alone, and he gave the same concern to everyone.

Cooperation and Client Service

Speaking in retrospect, Doriot remarked on the cooperation that eventually came to the Military Planning Division: "We had the cooperation, friendship, and the respect of Army and other commanders.

We also had the cooperation of many people in industry, in science, the War Production Board and in the Congress. We had letters from generals . . . and others thanking us for our liaison men and observers, both on R&D [research and development] and requirements. These gentlemen and the men under their command were our clients and that was our attitude toward them."[28] How Doriot got things done within the division was an extension of this viewpoint. "You cannot order people to do things," he told a division member. "You have to sell them on the idea and let them go as far as they can."[29]

During the war, Doriot wrote to a division field observer in a combat zone, "I have read with very much interest all your letters. I am particularly happy that whenever you have the opportunity you pay attention to the Air Forces, the Marines and the Navy. Indeed we must help everyone any time in any way. Be quite certain to tell me anything you might need and keep on advising us as to suggestions we should follow. . . . Do not hesitate to let me know whatever you want that we do not do fast enough or do not do right."[30]

At war's end, the division's contribution in superior food, clothing and equipment was a significant factor in the lower number of U.S. casualties in comparison to fatalities suffered by other nations. The QM Corps is truly one of the great success stories. The Military Planning Division's methods early in World War II in integration, coordination and an attitude of service are particularly relevant today.

Update

In 1954 the Natick Laboratories was dedicated to the achievement of Doriot's vision of an "Institute of Man" to continue to build on his inter-disciplinary wartime research. The Army values demonstrated in World War II efforts continued. In the words of Mary Mandels, a pioneer and longtime researcher, "We did not have jobs—we had a calling."[31]

In 1967 the Army recognized Doriot's contribution as founder of the organization at Natick. The ceremonies acknowledged the 25 years of unprecedented mutual cooperation for the combat soldier between the national scientific and industrial communities and Army enterprise.[32]

Marcia L. Lightbody retired as an editor and historian at the U.S. Army Soldier Systems Center, Natick, Massachusetts. This article is adapted from a presentation at the 1998 Conference of Army Historians, Beltsville, Maryland, sponsored by the U.S. Army Center of Military History.

Notes

1. Stephen J. Kennedy, quoted in "The Beginnings of Quartermaster Research and Development," paper written to author (Natick, MA: 1988), 2.

2. Russell Davis in personal communication to author, August 1995.

3. Richard Testa in personal communication to author, August 1994.

4. Georges Frederic Doriot: A Register of His Papers, U.S. Library of Congress, Manuscript Division, Washington, D.C., 1992.

5. Smithsonian Institution unedited symposium videotape, "Outfitted to Fight in World War II," Washington, D.C., August 1995.

6. Kennedy, 2.

7. Doriot, dinner address in *Proceedings*, Founder's Day, Commemoration of 25 Years of Army Research and Development for the Combat Soldier, Natick, MA, 7-8 December 1967, 107.

8. Robert Bates, *The Love of the Mountains Is Best* (Portsmouth, NH: Peter E. Randall, Publisher, 1994), 210.

9. Smithsonian videotape.

10. Edward Heller in personal communication to author, May 1998.

11. "Lieut. Col. Georges Doriot's Ingenuity Helps Army Save Quantities of Vital Materials," *The Washington Post* (7 June 1942, section B); Heller, August 1995.

12. David B. Dill, Robert E. Johnson, Robert M. Kark, "Feeding Problems in Man as Related to Environment," Report 3 to Committee on Food Research, Quartermaster Food and Container Institute of the Armed Forces, Cambridge, MA, Fatigue Laboratory, June 1946.

13. Elton Burgett in personal communication to author, August 1995.

14. *The Washington Post.*

15. Burgett, 1998.

16. Dill, *Harvard Fatigue Laboratory Reports*, 1 (July 1940-June 1941), 4.

17. Bates, in personal communication to author, May 1998.

18. Bates, *The Love of Mountains*, 185-86.

19. Ibid., 206.

20. Emil M. Mrak, "Feeding the Combat Soldier," *Proceedings*, Founder's Day, 36.

21. *The Washington Post.*

22. David R. Peryam, "Sensory Evaluation—The Early Days," *Food Technology* (January 1990), 87.

23. Doriot, dinner address, 103.

24. Ibid., 107.

25. Heller, May 1998.

26. Doriot, memorandum to Gregory, 31 March 1943.

27. Ibid., dinner address, 108.

28. Ibid.

29. Heller in Smithsonian videotape, August 1995.

30. Isabelle Pounder in Smithsonian videotape, August 1995.

31. Mary Mandels, remarks, Hall of Fame Induction Ceremony, Natick, MA, 6 November 1998.

32. William O. Baker, in Foreword, *Proceedings*, Founder's Day, 1967.

THE EDUCATOR

FROM CAMBRIDGE, MASSACHUSETTS TO FONTAINEBLEU:

The Beginnings of INSEAD

WHEN GEORGES DORIOT began teaching at the Harvard Business School in 1928, the American economy was about to enter one of its most turbulent periods in recent memory. It was the year that Herbert Hoover was elected president of the United States, following the presidency of Calvin Coolidge.

In his March 4, 1925, inaugural, in the wake of the disastrous presidency of Warren G. Harding riddled with corruption in Washington, Coolidge declared that the nation had achieved "a state of contentment seldom before seen." The prosperous years of the Coolidge era followed, with revenues pouring in and the federal government barely enlarging its services.

Coolidge's thoughts on the American economy are revealing: "What we need is thrift and industry. . . . The man who builds a factory builds a temple. . . . The man who works there worships there. . . . Large profits mean large payrolls. . . ."

On the role of government Coolidge said: "If the Federal govern-ment should go out of existence, the common run of people would not detect the difference in the affairs of their daily life for a considerable length of time....The business of America is business."

A new faith in business was taking hold of the American mind, prompted in part by the World War I production miracles and in part by the clever new writings of American public-relations experts and advertising men. But the plight of the average worker improved little during this time. Although real wages increased about 26 percent from 1919 to 1929, the average worker earned less than $1,500 at a time when $1,800 was estimated as a requirement for a minimum decent living standard. Ironically, union membership declined from over five million in 1920 to four and a third million in 1929.

Georges Doriot belonged to a milieu which believed, among other things, in the role of business in improving people's lives. In the surge of enthusiasm which often propels products to markets, the quality of life of workers—not as potential consumers, but as actual fabricators of the product—is often forgotten. Given his working class upbringing in France, and his unstinted admiration of hard-working people engaged on the production line, Doriot's view of work was very inclusive.

Georges Doriot began teaching at the Harvard Business School in 1928. During the nearly four decades that followed, ending with his retirement from Harvard in 1966, Doriot engaged with the world of capitalists, managers, and consumers as much as he did with the world of ordinary working-class people.

The conditions under which he retired are a matter of interpreta-tion. Suffice it to say that he wasn't happy about leaving and somewhat unhappier about the direction that HBS was taking. While Doriot clearly enjoyed the spotlight that HBS provided, he also felt that the teaching was too iconoclastic and without imagination. And in many of his remarks to alumni and students he seemed to indicate that HBS students were preparing for anointed roles in business rather than learning to be effective businessmen.

The idea for INSEAD came to Doriot in the War years but there was no way to put it into action. In the years immediately following World War II, reconstruction took precedence over the implementation of new ideas.

It was during the aftermath of World War I that Doriot became an avid student of the Dawes Plan for the reconstruction of Europe and a critic of many of the economic strategies that were put in place. He also became a fervent globalist, realizing well ahead of many of the businessmen of the time that there was a world economy in place—and that no nation could shield itself from the major trends that shaped this world economy. The world was changing and the solutions needed to succeed in that world needed to be as malleable as that changing world. He perceived the need for a business teaching environment that was global and iterative, that took its cues not from a set of predetermined texts but improvised as it went along.

But Europe didn't have a tradition of business schools and certainly nothing close to what Doriot may have visualized. And there wasn't a strategy that Doriot could come up with that would create INSEAD in the manner in which he wanted it created.

Ironically, it was the promise of an HBS-like institution that became the selling point for INSEAD. Ironic, because Doriot wanted INSEAD to be a global stage rather than American. And he wanted the practice of business as taught at INSEAD to be more populist than at HBS. But Harvard was the only point of reference that had any resonance for the French and the authorities that Doriot was selling the concept to.

The roots of INSEAD can be traced to a more modest institution— the *Centre de Perfectionnment aux Affaires* (*CPA*)—that began in October of 1930 in Paris. The initial idea was to create a postgraduate program that would help college graduates make the transition to business. What *CPA* became instead was a middle-management program that drew heavily on case studies as taught at Harvard and focused on training managers and engineers for further advancement in business.

CPA was financed by the Paris Chamber of Commerce, the French government and student contributions. At the time it started, students paid about 3,000 francs in annual fees or about the average of a monthly salary for starting managers.

Jean-Louis Barsoux, in his excellent history *INSEAD: From Intuition to Institution* describes the importance of CPA for INSEAD in the following manner . . .

> Understanding the historical development of the CPA is relevant for the story that follows. Several features are worth highlighting: the fact that the CPA represented a successful collaboration between Doriot and the Paris Chamber of Commerce; the role of Harvard as a source of educational material, inspiration and legitimacy; the fact that the CPA was a post-experience school, where teaching was based on the case method and group work; the early experience with fee-paying education which was virtually unknown in Europe at the time. These parallels are important: first, because they show how the CPA helped pave the way for the later creation of INSEAD; second, because they show that INSEAD was neither a blinding flash of vision nor a stroke of sheer luck, but rather a thoughtful development on a successful initiative. In many ways the CPA represented a kind of dry run for the ambitious undertaking that was to follow—and would also prove a tremendous source of technical support.

In the twenty-five years since its founding, the CPA became an important European venue for the teaching of management not only because of its uniqueness, but also because of the subject matter it encompassed. It helped bring a more customized—call it European— understanding of the problems that its students faced. And its reputation, along with Doriot's own growing stature as teacher, a war strategist, and a visionary, became the driving arguments for INSEAD.

INSEAD was no extension of CPA, it was to be its own entity— a European business school that would be based in Europe but not exclusively for Europe. Indeed, Doriot wanted to draw on the global business community for INSEAD's teachers and its students. Notes Barsoux:

On 13 June 1955, Doriot made his first public presentation of the project at the CPA. In the fortnight that followed the presentation Doriot met two leading French business figures to tell them more about his project. They were Raoul de Vitry d'Avaucourt, president of Pechiney (with whom he had remained very close since a first meeting in 1939) and Hely d'Oissel, president of Saint Gobain (succeeded two years later by Arnaud de Vogue). As Doriot later recalled, these individuals, with their powerful business, social and political connections were key "recruits" to the cause. "They gave their time, their support, their reputations. I made several speeches. They were always there. Again, without Doriot's high-level connections and capacity to persuade busy people to give up their time and use their influence, the idea might simply never have gathered momentum.

On 13 July 1955, the Paris Chamber of Commerce held a big meeting to discuss Doriot's proposal in more detail—this time inviting important figures from outside France, notably Bertrand Fox, vice-dean of Harvard Business School and Thomas H. Carroll, the vice-president of the Ford Foundation (who also happened to be head of the Harvard Business School alumni association). Unfortunately, Doriot himself was unable to attend. An additional point of interest emerged at this stage concerning the site: Doriot's recommendation was that the school should be "established outside but near Paris" for the convenience of visiting instructors flying in from abroad.

The assembled parties strongly supported the idea of the school, considering that many of the implementation difficulties (to do with the cross-national nature of the project) were actually arguments in its favour and speculating that, once established, the school would "prove not only useful but indispensable." This meeting was significant in that the idea was starting to make its way without Doriot's physical presence.

It took another two years before the Paris Chamber of Commerce finally committed itself to the idea of INSEAD. At its annual general meeting held on July 5, 1957, the Chamber announced that it would help establish an European business school, in effect agreeing to under-write the costs of the start-up.

In one of the subsequent INSEAD publications, Doriot had this to say about the geography and the philosophy behind INSEAD, the "direction" of management, sense of perfection, the sense of action, the sense of the future, and seizing the opportunity :

During the first years of INSEAD, we had to find a location and thought of the Fontainebleau Chateau. We were informed that the rooms of the palace were, in principle, reserved for "artistic" endeavors and not "busi-ness." We obtained satisfaction, however, by demonstrating that manag-ing a business was, indeed, an "art" and that employing computers and management techniques alone would never constitute a "science."

In truth, it is possible to acquire a veneer of business, with time and money, but doesn't the grandeur of human beings reside in the heart and not the brain? Has teaching killed off the essential qualities of "courage" and "initiative"? Some people pretend that we must descend into the street to rediscover them. This business school was conceived with the intent of assembling and sublimating these qualities of heart, courage, and initiative.

Direction of Management:

We say "business administration"; we should rather speak of direc-tion of management. If we consider a business like a ball in a game of football (soccer), it is subject to external forces. Once the goals have been fixed, the ball is directed toward the goal, taking into account the reactions of the adversary and, sometimes, making use of them. But, even here, the choice of the management team must be considered primordial, as well as that of the people outside the business who must collaborate with the internal team.

As with human capital, there is also a production asset which one needs to know how to procure over the long term, and that is the "credit" of the business. This is a kind of premium on the quality of the work performed.

At the management level, the act of management itself can be separated into "management," "leadership," and "command." In a critical situation, the decision, once taken, is applied without discussion. This is the command. Management and leadership are necessary at different levels of management and in different, more daily, situations.

Sense of Perfection

The sense of perfection concerns us both as an individual and as a member of the group. For each one, a dialogue with oneself is essential. A notebook of confidential notes allows this dialogue, this reflection, which becomes a mirror of the self.

In the path to perfection, have you noticed, for example, the extraordinary force of marginal effort? That which we must do as we attempt to attain perfection, the moment "Epsilon" that is reserved for helping and listening. This effort "Epsilon" is the essential motor of generosity. The habit of giving is a major trump card in teamwork: to learn when to speak, to speak neither too soon nor too late; in a word: to know when to contribute.

The Sense of Action

We are surrounded by specialists and analysts. This is not the only objective of teaching. For, if you learn to analyze at the Institute, you must also know how to bring the effort of reflection to its finality which is action. Without a sense of action, the world would still be at the stage of the idea. Reflection must be "action bent."

The Sense of the Future

The vision of the future is today an essential condition to the survival of the enterprise. Look at the great entrepreneurs of the past 20 years. They have played a capital role in the evolution of the company. This vision of the future leads the head of the enterprise to be conscious of his role in the company. The company of tomorrow depends on his wit/spirit and generosity.

The sense of the future asks of the individual to know how to adapt to changes of which he is conscious. For you, it is important to know how to conform, but also at times to reform.

Seizing the Opportunity

You are going to receive an exceptional education; you will one day be asked what you have accomplished with it.

A bird flies by; few people notice. This is opportunity. Be among those who seize the opportunity.

Doriot's vision for INSEAD, shaped no doubt by his experiences as a teacher, as a venture capitalist investing in the future of technology, and as a problem-solver in the U.S. Army, was of an entrepreneurial business environment in which risk-taking and innovation were rewarded. John Whitehead, the Goldman Sachs executive and one of the many who studied in his Manufacturing class, reminds us that although Doriot taught at Harvard Business School—where the case-study method was the only language—Doriot never used the case method. Indeed, a great deal of the INSEAD vision was conceptualized to counter the pedagogical rigidity that Doriot seemed to rile against in his later years.

INSEAD

Created, Supported by French Enterprise

THE NEW EUROPEAN
BUSINESS SCHOOL

(from French Actuelle, Vol. VIII, No. 21 December 1, 1959)

IT IS A BRISK LATE FALL AFTERNOON, and out along the ancient cobblestoned court of the beautiful Fontainebleau Chateau amble clusters of young men with briefcases, speaking earnestly together in German, French, English. Though they have emerged from the Louis XV wing of the venerable Chateau, their talk is not of the history and art treasures left behind by Francis I, the Napoleons and Other French Greats, nor even of modern Greats, but of incongruous matters like product development, time studies, financial structures, market testing, stockholder relations. . . . For they are sixty young men who have pointed their future careers and contributions toward helping shape and direct the productive and trading institutions and arrangements of the new Europe: They are the first class of the first year of the triple-titled *Institut Europeen d'Administration des Affaires—* European Institute of Business Administration—*Europäisches Institut für Betriebsfuhrung.*

These serious-minded young men have come to the famed town of

Fontainebleau to study at the new graduate school created by the combined vision and effort of the French Chamber of Commerce in Paris, the Harvard School of Business Administration, the European Productivity Agency, French private enterprise, and other European and American supporters. In it, they will receive the groundwork training and understanding that should start them off soundly toward becoming enlightened and leading executives in the business enterprises of the fast-developing European Economic Community.

THE AMERICAN BACKGROUND

Clearly European in its orientation and direction, the new Institute is just as admittedly American-patterned in its organization and method. The genesis was nicely reported and phrased by the New York Herald Tribune's economic expert, Jan Hasbrouck, who recently wrote: "Ever since the war the fraternity of old grads of the Harvard School of Business Administration has been growing steadily in the boardrooms and counting houses of Europe. These forward-looking young men have often regretted that no university in Europe has so far been willing to regard business as a profession and to set up a graduate school to turn out pre-tailored tycoons."

This situation has now been remedied. The director of the Institute at Fontainebleau, tall, poised Olivier Giscard d'Estaing, is himself a 1951 graduate of the Harvard School of Business Administration. The Harvard School, in fact, from the very beginning has given its assistance and support to the European Institute, and loaned its well-known Industrial Management Professor, Georges F. Doriot, as chief counselor in setting up the new school and starting it off on the right track. Accordingly, the school's method of instruction is based largely on the Harvard system of case discussion.

Three of the school's professors and two of its students are Americans, and a personal financial contribution toward starting the Institute was made by Mr. Thomas E. Cougdon of Denver, Colorado. As for American moral support, the list of well-wishers is headed by President Dwight D. Eisenhower, who sent his greetings on the school's opening day; and by his assistant, General Wilton B. Persons, who wrote: "As an alumnus of the Harvard Business School, I know how important this enterprise can be to the future of the European Community. Its faculty and students will play a creative role in the economic affairs of their area—and indeed throughout the world."

FRENCH AND OTHER EUROPEAN SUPPORT

The French business community has given the project indispensable support and funds. It was the Paris Chamber of Commerce, above all, that pushed ahead with the idea and provided the fundamental support for the Institute's founding and operation. To set things in motion, the Paris Chamber last year contributed the franc equivalent of $20,000, and this year has given $40,000.

The *Conseil National du Patronat Francais* (Federation of French Industries) has also contributed substantially to the Institute's budget. And of the twenty business and banking enterprises which have made considerable contributions to the school's fund, two are Dutch and eighteen are French.

As for the 53 European and American leaders in education, government and business who have agreed to give their full support to the new Institute, 21 are French. Among those backing the school: Vernon R. Alden, associate dean of the Harvard School; Joseph Beck, Foreign Minister of Luxembourg; Walter Boveri, president of the Swiss firm of Brown, Boveri & Co.; Louis Camu, president of the Bank of Brussels;

Dr. Walter Hallstein, president of the Commission of the European Economic Community; Etienne Hirsch, president of Euratom; Paul Rijkens, former president of Holland's Unilever Company; Robert Schumann, president of the European Parliament in Strasbourg and former French prime minister; Paul-Henri Spaak, secretary-general of NATO; M.V. Valletta, president of the Italian Fiat Company; Georges Villiers, president of the Federation of French Industries; Arnaud de Vogue, president of the French Saint-Gobain Company.

The International Chamber of Commerce and O.E.E.C.'s European Productivity Agency (EPA) are also behind the Institute. The EPA, indeed, is said by the school's Administration to have given "especially great help." And the French Ministry of Culture, headed by writer Andre Malraux, has provided the Fontainebleau Chateau quarters for the school at "a very nominal rent."

A EUROPEAN ENTERPRISE

The "European" focus of the Institute is set forth appropriately in the official prospectus: "The foundation of the new Institute is fundamentally European, and its development is closely linked to the economic integration of Europe. This has been the basis for the choice of its curriculum, undergraduate body, faculty, and languages used.

"The Institute has been organized for European enterprise, and therefore it is natural that European enterprise has been mostly responsible for the financing, provision of instructors, selection of subjects to be studied, and planned practicability of the whole program.

"The Institute's Research Department, oriented toward a study of the problems raised for European enterprise by European integration, is at the disposition of any company wishing to have data or documentation in this field.

"By turning out a new class of young businessmen each year—

graduates imbued with a spirit of good European cooperation and well-informed on the currents of contemporary business and its practices—the Institute fills a very real and present need of the commercial, industrial and banking enterprises of Europe."

Spelling this out in practical educational terms, Director d'Estaing says the cases the students discuss in the Harvard manner are constructed with a far-seeing eye toward the development of European business in the framework of a closely cooperating and economically integrating European Community. (And d'Estaing himself likes to think ahead in terms of an eventual European co-operation and Common Market still bigger than the six-nation Economic Community.) Courses and field trips will also serve to familiarize the students with various individual enterprises and with local methods of management, marketing, finance and production in the present national areas.

Comments the Herald Tribune's Jan Hasbrouck: "The reasons why this new school has been greeted with such enthusiasm should be obvious to anyone who has looked ahead at the inevitable development of Europe's economy over the next generation. The techniques developed at Harvard, and the very concept of a business school, would have had little meaning to the limited, established, static, often family-owned businesses of Europe's past. But expansion into a prospective continental market, increased competition, and rapid expansion have already made the methods developed in the United States for similar conditions highly pertinent here.

"The graduates of the new school will not only be versed in these techniques, but they will also be 'European' businessmen. They will know languages, conditions and problems throughout Europe, and, incidentally, will have made many contacts among students of other nationalities which cannot help but be useful later on. It is interesting to note that two of the students are Americans whose idea is to fit themselves as executives of European branches of American corporations."

THE STUDENT BODY

Out of 130 applicants, 60 were accepted for the Institute's first class, which convened on September 14. Of the groups, 30 are from France, seven from Germany, six from Italy, three from Belgium, three from Luxembourg, two from the Netherlands, two from the United States (Joseph Candiotti, a Mexico City University graduate from Seattle, Washington; and Claus Leuthold, a Harvard graduate from Lexington, Massachusetts), and one each from Austria, Hungary, Morocco, Norway, Spain, Switzerland, and the United Kingdom. All have university degrees, and some have already held positions in business. The youngest is 20-year-old Anthony Belfield, a graduate of Manchester University in England, and the oldest, 39-year-old Horst Behr, a graduate of Munich University in West Germany.

SELECTION

An applicant for admission to the Institute fills out a questionnaire, and then is nominated or rejected by a Committee in his home country to go to the Institute for a long personal interview by the Admissions Committee.

Selection is made on the basis of scholastic record, extra-curricular accomplishment, working record (if any), and aptitude for leadership. After this first 1959-1960 school year, it is hoped to hold representation from any one country to a maximum 30 percent of the student body, and, as a general rule, to admit young men between the ages of 21 and 28.

At present, women are not being considered for admission to the Institute.

COSTS

The fee Jar for each student is 700,000 francs (about $1,400), and this includes tuition, lodging, laundry, and food for the ten-month school year. If the student or his family is unable to pay the full amount, he may receive a partial scholarship or an honor loan which is to be paid within five years after graduation.

FACULTY

Instruction is given by faculty professors, associate professors, and assistant professors. Twelve are French, and German, three American—Professor of Marketing Paul Dulaney Converse from the University of Illinois, Professor of Finance Wilford John Eiteman from the University of Michigan, and Assistant Professor of Business Policy Stanley Hillyer, a business consultant with offices in Boston and five European capitals and there is one each from Belgium, Canada, Egypt, the Netherlands, Switzerland, and the United Kingdom.

Salaries are paid according to professorial rank and standing. The salaries of the American professors, incidentally, are entirely paid by the European Productivity Agency, with the school meeting local expenses at Fontainebleau.

CURRICULUM

Courses are given in Marketing, Production, Finance, Control and Accounting, Human Relations, Business Policy, and in the Economic, Social and Institutional Framework of Europe.

To "form businessmen able to adapt themselves rapidly and effectively to the life of an enterprise" lectures and discussions will cover all business activities—financing, accounting, statistics, production, sales, human relations, and management policy. To "prepare these business-men for their European mission" each course will be "directed toward solution of problems raised by the diversity of methods and traditions of the individual European nations." And the special course in the European economic and social framework "will familiarize students with the structure of European institutions and will give them practical ideas about the general problems created by the cooperative organiza-tion of the European economy."

The "human relations" seems to extend only to management-labor and inter-enterprise relations. When a reporter asked the school's admin-istration why there is no course in the theory and practice of modern public relations, including community and consumer aspects, market research, contact with representatives of radio, press, television, and other opinion-molders, and advertising techniques, it appeared there was no real awareness of the importance of this side of successful enterprise and market-making in the world today. Yet it is evident to those who know contemporary U.S. business—as indeed it has been to French and other European graduate students who have made study tours of the United States in recent years—that it is in the field of merchandising and public relations that European enterprise perhaps has most to learn from America. The Directors, however, said they hope to meet this lack by having some special lectures and discussions on the subject.

Since classes and seminars are conducted only in French, German and English, students admitted to the Institute are required to know one of these languages perfectly, another well, and the third to some extent. For those weak in one of the languages, there is a special three-week course of intensive language study prior to the opening of the fall session.

STUDY SYSTEM

The teaching relies heavily on the Harvard-developed "case method," concentrating on analysis and discussion. Frequently, businessmen from specific sectors of the economy are called in to talk of their fields of industrial activity and their individual work. "Group study, discussion and solution of a problem are emphasized in order to habituate the future businessmen of Europe to working as a team with other nationalities." And "visits to factories, banks and offices are organized, and individual or group reports prepared along the lines of problems and possibilities raised in the adaptation of these enterprises to the Common Market."

"CAMPUS" LIFE

The students are housed in two buildings near the Chateau, one a former hotel and the other a former private mansion. They live one, two, and in a few cases three to a room or suite. In between the two buildings is a dining hall. The chef is French, and there seems to be general enjoyment of the food. (Wine is available at an extra charge.)

Certain indispensable books for the courses and seminars are provided free, but if the student wants to keep the volume he must pay for it. A library is well filled with useful background books.

Morning classes are held from 9:00 to 11:45, lunch is from 12:00 to 12:45, an afternoon lecture may be given from 1:15 to 2:30, and then seminars start, "extending as long into the evening as the students like." Dinner is from 7:00 to 8:30, depending on length of the case discussions.

Weekends are free, and for those who wish there is riding, tennis, fencing or Ping-Pong. Students may leave Fontainebleau on weekends, and about 60 percent of them so far this year have been going off to see the sights and historic places of Paris and other parts of France. The school term begins in the middle of September and continues until the Christmas recess. Classes commence again on January 4 and, except for a ten-day Easter break, go on to early June. There are stiff oral and written examinations, and those who pass receive diplomas. Then, until the middle of July, the students visit factories and commercial enterprises with their instructors for on-the-spot examinations and talks with engineers and business executives.

A BRIGHT FUTURE

Able and practical-minded W. Chr. Posthumus Meyjes, former Dutch Ambassador to Greece, who has been appointed director-general of the new Institute, is pleased with its progress to date, and optimistic about its future. In charge of the school's general organization and fund-raising, he has received, apart from tuition fees, 67 million francs in the past year from businessmen and companies about 99 percent of it from French sources. He feels that outside support, however, will have to average something like 200 million francs a year if the hoped-for annual student body of 150 is to be properly taught, housed and fed.

Says Posthumus Meyjes: "I think we'll get it, because so far the support has been even more favorable than I had expected. As for the school itself, the amalgamation of the many nationalities has been most rapid, and the students have been making good suggestions about the work program. Also, we are developing a team spirit among the Institute's' directors, faculty and students. As for next year's class, inquiries are now coming in at the rate of three a day."

Director of the Institute Olivier Giscard d'Estaing, younger brother of the French Secretary of State for Finance, says: "So far, we are meeting the normal reaction to the case system. Some of the students are enthusiastic, some find it difficult and different from what they expected and feel a bit lost. But certainly we are breaking down the nationalistic approach. We are living together in international working groups of seven, which gives the students a new cosmopolitan ease and a non-chauvinistic and co-operative approach. All of them are pleased to be in actual, practical contact with business life and problems. We are making good progress as pioneers in a new European business community."

Graduates, says d'Estaing, will not have any trouble landing jobs; in fact, he thinks they will be able to pick and choose among the leading enterprises of Europe which are looking forward to the day when their one big free market will consist of at least 165 million consumers.

POSTSCRIPT

General Doriot followed very closely the development of INSEAD over the years until the very end of his life and was an active adviser to the three chairman, Jean Marcou, John Loudon and Claude Janssen. He lectured quite often and many INSEAD students were directly acquainted with his thinking about business life.

The library on the campus in Fontainebleau is named the "Georges and Edna Doriot Information Center" and was partially financed by DEC. There is an excellent sculpture of the General and a plaque bearing a hallmark quote from him, "Without action, the world would still be an idea."

Forty-five years after its beginning, INSEAD has become one of the top business schools in the world and is usually considered as the top school outside the U.S., certainly the most global with two campuses in Fontainebleau and Singapore. The MBA classes number 850 per year. INSEAD is the largest provider of executive education in the world, it has a Ph.D. program and a permanent faculty of 150.

The principles that were set up before the school started are still applied, because INSEAD is completely international, independent and entrepreneurial. The spirit of the General when he founded INSEAD has been maintained by the General's lieutenants: Olivier Giscard d'Estaing, who after managing the school from 1959 to 1966, was vice chairman of the board from 1969 to 1994 and is currently chairman of the INSEAD Foundation, and Claude Janssen, who, after being involved in many aspects of the founding of the school, was executive vice chairman from 1971 to 1982 and then chairman of the board from 1982 to 2004.

The dream of the General has came true, even beyond the wildest expectations of its founders and INSEAD is an extraordinary proof of his impressive vision.

DORIOT BY DORIOT
FROM BEAULIEU TO BOSTON

Interview with General Georges F. Doriot by Aulikki Olsen

The life of Georges Doriot covered an amazing span of our social and political history which saw the decline of the great European imperialist powers, the rise and decline of European Communism, the transformation of Asia, and the emergence of the United States as the world's undisputed super-power. America's dominance in international affairs went hand in hand with its enviable record of industrial and technological supremacy. What makes Georges Doriot's life unquestionably deserving of our interest is the role it played in shaping a significant part of this evolution as it flowed through the social vision of the Roosevelt era into the decidedly more capitalistic ideology of the last fifty years.

Ken Olsen, the founding spirit behind Digital Equipment Corporation— also the most successful investment of Doriot's venture capital fund— remained a lifelong friend and admirer of Doriot. In the 1980s, Aulikki Olsen, wife of Ken Olsen, started a series of conversations with Doriot. From those conversations, and in Doriot's own words, we catch a glimpse of an amazing life, a life that began in the idyllic eastern region of France between the Jura Mountains and the River Doubs and ended on the U.S. East Coast.

I WAS BORN IN PARIS ON SEPTEMBER TWENTY-FOURTH, 1899. My father and mother had moved to Paris very shortly before that time. Our family came from a beautiful village in eastern France right at the corner of

Switzerland, an area that was at the time Germany. The city nearest to the village where father and mother stayed was Mouillevillers.

Valentigney is an absolutely beautiful village with hills and many trees on a very attractive river called the Doubs. It is a very old part of France. Many of the villages around were occupied and built by the Romans. As a matter of fact, in the next village which is now called Beaulieu you can still find Roman ruins of buildings and viaducts. The village was built of stone houses with red roof tiles. Every house had a wall around it high enough to protect it but not so high that you could not look over and see the flowers, beautiful gardens and many birds. I remember it with a great deal of feeling. It is one of the most beautiful villages I have ever seen anywhere.

It was a completely Protestant district. As a matter of fact, when I was young there was no Catholic Church in the village. Most of the people were farmers, but many of them also worked in the factory owned by the Peugeot Company. They made kitchenware and, later on, made bicycles and tricycles. Most members of my family worked there. At least the men worked there. The women, while taking care of their homes, would go to the factory with a little pushcart and get some tools and different things that they would bring home and work at home whenever they had a minute to spare.

I also remember what was called the Fraternelle. The Fraternelle was a cooperative store owned by the Peugeot Company. Every morning a member of the family would take one of her nice little pushcarts and go to the Fraternelle. When you got within a few hundred yards there was a wonderful smell of freshly baked bread, coffee, and many other things. The trips to the Fraternelle are one of the most pleasant recollections of my life. Everyone knew each other and everyone was very kind and helpful to each other. Whenever anyone was in need, there would always be a neighbor to come and help.

Father was the next-to-the-youngest child of eight or nine, I do not remember. Mother was the youngest of about that many. Mother came from a neighboring village, not far from Valentigney. As far as I can remember, father was born in another village called San Suzanne, while my mother was born in Vandoncourt. My grandfather was a farmer, not a large farmer, but enough of a farmer to be able to live and build his own home—which he probably did with his own hands as most of the people did at that time—and then bring up his children. We all went to school.

I used to go to Valentigney and spend my vacations there. Somehow, most of my vacation time was spent with my girl cousins because they had more time. They were older and they were all very very sweet to me. Some of father's brothers moved away from the village, but his sisters married there and stayed there. I remember with great affection my aunts, especially Tante Lucy and Tante Juliette. They were all very hard-working people. Tante Lucy's husband was the local captain (a sort of leader of the working people). He was a heavy-set man, and again very hard working.

Once more, my overwhelming recollection of that period is the beauty of the village, the kindness of the people toward one another, and also that they were very hard working. In the summer, men requested permission to be able to start work at four or five o'clock in the morning so that they could spend the afternoon taking care of their fields and gardens. Then, at night we would all sit quietly together, talk peacefully, and be grateful for what we had.

It was a wonderful world. People were not rich; they had to work for everything they had. They went to church very regularly and the Protestant minister was a kind and very respected man with a good education. So, I speak very feelingly about Valentigney. In the course of time, the Peugeot factory became larger and other factories opened up downstream on the river. The Peugeot factory started making bicycles and tricycles.

Father was a mechanic and apparently an extremely good one. In or about 1887, father and his cousin who was an engineer, went to Germany and purchased a Daimler engine. I think it was a Daimler engine number 2. It was a V-type engine with about 2½ horsepower, I think. They placed it on a tricycle and broke its neck, so they placed a fourth wheel on the tricycle and called it a quadricycle, and that was one of the very first automobiles made with the name quadricycle, not the name automobile. The engine was in the rear. Later on, they transferred the engine to the front.

When father was asked many years later why he had done that, he said that he did not want to. In fact, he wanted to keep the engine in the rear. The name of the engine at that time was "explosion" engine. People did not like the feeling that an explosion engine was sitting right under them. Furthermore, they were accustomed to a horse pulling them and could not quite comprehend why, if the engine had replaced the horse, why the engine wasn't in front. So the engine went to the front even though father did not think it was a very good idea.

The archives of the Peugeot company record that a Serpollet-Peugeot steam-powered tricycle was presented at the Universal Exhibition in 1889. According to these records, it was probably the first vehicle one could call an automobile. This vehicle is what gave rise to driving permits in Paris, and the Serpollet obtained the very first of these. Next, the manufacturers came up with the gasoline-powered quadricycle, which could reach 24 kilometers per hour. This vehicle was produced in association with a friend of the Peugeots, Emile Levassor, who held an exclusive contract for Gottlieb-Daimler motors in France.

Interestingly, the Peugeot archives also note that, in 1894, the Paris-Rouen race organized by the "Petit Journal," was won by a petrol-powered Peugeot quadricycle driven by a Doriot.

But back to Georges. . . .

After father and mother were married, which happened rather late in life—I think father was over thirty when he was married—they were transferred to Paris. In the western part of Paris, Mr. Armand Peugeot had a house. It was Number 7. There was this house and a stable which was transformed into a garage. Mr. and Mrs. Armand Peugeot lived on the first floor and my father and mother, who worked for Mr. Peugeot, lived on the second floor, and that is where I was born.

It seems that during that period, most of the people who purchased a car were well-to-do, well-known people who lived in Paris. Apparently, they had to have father in Paris to show them how to drive a car, and then to take care of repairs and maintenance. Well, the family therefore had to live in Paris. Later, we moved to Nurgi which was a very short distance from where I was born. Eventually, father left the Peugeot Company and went to work for another automobile company for a very short period, and then started making cars of his own.

My father's very first factory was in Nurgi. My sister, Madeline Joillet, was born in Nurgi. I went to school in Nurgi. After a while, about 1914, father's factory was transferred a little further west and father built a little home at Number 7 rue Franklin. My family lived there all their life, and my sister and her husband live there now, and that is where I stay when I go to Europe.

I went to school in Coubert-7, to the public school there. I can't say that I enjoyed it. I never enjoyed going to school because I was always afraid of not doing well and saddening my father and mother, particularly my father. My father was a very wonderful person, extremely quiet, very thoughtful, very kind, but very strong. He was a terribly hard worker. When he was young—I know this from my mother—he had worked as many as twelve to fourteen hours a day and he had still kept on doing that. When I was older, I realized how much he was doing. Father would seldom scold me, but the way he looked when he was not too pleased with me was much more effective than the scolding.

I owe him a great deal and, even now, I often say to myself, "What would Father think I should do?"

I went to church. But in France, at that time, one did not go to school on Thursday, so there was what we call Sunday school on Thursday morning, and then Sunday school on Sunday morning. I had a very wonderful pastor, Monsieur Besson. I made my First Communion and Confirmation at the local church. Later on, I went to college in Paris.

At that time, Father would allow me to go to the factory—which was very close to home—whenever I had time to do so. Schoolwork was very demanding. We were in school from 8:30 in the morning, came home for lunch for about one hour, and then went to school until 5 o'clock. We then had a great deal of homework to do. I remember vividly sitting at night in our living room—which was also the dining room—Father and Mother, my sister Zette (that was a name she was known by, it came from Joillet) and I, Father reading and working, Mother knitting or repairing clothes, and my sister and I working on our homework. We usually had at least two hours of homework every night. I remember the kerosene lamp over the table. It was one of those nice lamps that you could raise up and down as you wished.

So I remember my youth, so to speak, as being very close to my family. I loved my sister and had complete love, devotion and admiration for Father and Mother. I was a little bit of a mechanic and very early in life I turned out to be a fairly good draftsman. My main interest was reading American magazines having to do with machine tools and factory problems. I remember two American magazines in particular, one called *The American Machinist* which had a blue cover, and another called *Machinery* which was thicker and had a yellow cover.

I enjoyed driving cars and obtained my driver's license about a week after I was fifteen years old, which was the youngest age at which you could get it at that time. I still have that license. It said that I was allowed to drive a car at 220 horsepower. In fact, it is still referred to as a "patrol." Speaking about cars, a young Mr. Riggelou, a gentlemen for whom Father was working, took a car in Valentigney—which, as I have said, was close to Germany—and drove it all the way to Brest, which is at the tip end of Brittany. The total distance covered was 2,500 kilometers including the return trip (which we did at an average speed of 15 kilometers per hour). The weight of the car was 1,200 pounds and it had but two cylinders, a V-type engine, four speeds forward, one reverse. It was hell at the time, but an outstanding, remarkable trip just the same. In some way you could think of it, later on, as what Lindbergh did but, of course, less dangerous. It was referred to at the time as the famous Trip Valentigney-Brest á retour, which means there and return.

Later on, many years later, a friend of ours asked Father what we had used for fuel and he said we had used a form of kerosene, sending some ahead to different railroad stationmasters on the way. But, he said very often when we had not yet arrived, the stationmaster was afraid to hold it for fear it may catch fire. Sometimes, he would go to something like a dry-cleaning establishment for clothes and use whatever liquid the people used to clean in the business.

There are many stories from Father and Mother about their experiences in driving cars around Paris at that time. Peasants would chase them with their whips, chickens would get killed, which made the peasants very mad. One day Father was driving around Paris with Mother and her car got stuck. Well, they thought that they would be lynched, but somehow they finally convinced people and they saved themselves from a complete lynching. In other words, one could say that cars were not at all welcome. They were noisy, dangerous and even horses didn't like the cars. However, as more cars were made, as we know, all of that has changed.

In 1914, World War I came. Father's factory was transformed into a shell-making factory. At that time, people worked twenty-four hours a day, and I think my dear father probably worked twenty-four hours a day as well. I was in school most of that time, but members of the family suffered greatly. The part of France we came from furnished France with some of the most outstanding soldiers, and the regiments from that part took heavy casualties. As a matter of fact, I think that all my first cousins were killed on both sides of the family. I was much younger and went in the Army only about a year before we ended the war. I was in the artillery in, what is called in America, an Ordnance Company. My regiment had 145-millimeter long-range guns. We were equipped with the most-powerful guns in the French Army at the time. We did not use horses; instead, we had tractors, and I must say that it was a very educational period of my life.

I also had my share of good luck. Before long, I had to replace the engineering officer in charge of the artillery, and I suppose they replaced him thinking I could do the job all right because of my experience in Father's factory. It was an interesting situation because most of the soldiers who worked with me were very experienced repairmen from the best companies in Paris. At first they were disciplined but very aloof, and would always ask me for very detailed orders as to what to do to repair a car. I knew very well that they knew better than I but, of course, I was being tested and that is why they wanted detailed orders. Somehow, I survived the test and ended up having a wonderful relationship with them. I benefited from my contact with those men, even though I had a great deal of experience in Father's factories. I liked those men; I liked the way they worked. We understood and respected each other, and I can say that it was useful time and, in many ways, a happy time. I made some friends there that I kept in contact with for many years. They were much older than I and, of course, they have left this world a long time ago.

The end of the war came and I went back to school. A friend of my father's told him that since I was so interested in anything connected with machinery, production, and tools, he should give serious thought to sending me to America. France, at that time, was not in good shape.

Things were very hard, and people had to readjust themselves. The human loss had been tremendous and it was indeed a very bad situation. Father decided that he would take steps to send me to America to study matters connected with machine tools, the making of things, how to produce, and then after awhile return to France and get a job.

Father had a friend who was quite an important person in what is called technical education in France. He suggested that I should be sent to the Massachusetts Institute of Technology. Steps were taken, the American University Union made the necessary arrangements, and on or about January 4, 1921, I came to this country on the SS Touraine of the French Line. My first night was at the Hotel Statler in New York where I was amazed by the double door which allowed men to put newspapers and packages inside the door which I could then open from my room.

I was in New York on a Sunday morning and in that space between the two doors I found several pounds of newspapers. I thought that, America being a very kind country, people realized that I had been at sea for a week and, therefore, had very nicely kept a week's newspapers for me to read upon my arrival. Much to my amazement, I discovered that those pounds of papers were just the Sunday edition of the American newspaper.

I came to Boston and stayed at the Hotel Tremont at the corner of Tremont and Boylston, and then went to MIT to register. The friend of Father's who worked for the Bankers Trust in Paris had given me a letter of introduction to a gentleman named A. Lawrence Lowell. On the envelope it merely said "A. Lawrence, Esquire." Having the letter to this gentleman by the name of Lowell, I decided that I should be considerate and polite, as my father and mother would have told me to be. So, before starting classes at MIT, I looked for him and found that he was president of a university called Harvard.

Well, I must say, that in my family we had never heard of Harvard. Now, of course, I feel I must apologize for that, but nevertheless that was the case. So, I called on Mr. A. Lawrence Lowell who was on the second floor of University Hall. He was extremely kind to me. He asked me what I wanted to learn and I told him that I wanted to learn how to run a factory. He smiled and said that I was going to the wrong place and that I should go to a place called the Harvard Business School. Whereupon, he took me downstairs in University Hall and introduced me to Wells B. Dunham, dean of the Harvard Business School. Dunham agreed that the ideal place for me was the Harvard Business School so papers were transferred from MIT to the Harvard Business School.

I spent a year at the Harvard Business School mostly studying Industrial Management, factory problems and systems, industrial accounting, labor relations, statistics, and corporate finance. I had very outstanding teachers, like Professor Callinan, Professor Dewing and Professor Sprague. I enjoyed the experience very much. At the end of that year I had met people in New York who offered me a job; I took it. In the meantime, I had come to France to visit the family and they decided that it was probably best for me to stay in the United States because people were very nice to me and I could probably earn a living. Things were not very happy in France at that time. We were still suffering from the aftereffects of World War I.

So, I came back and was working in New York. During that period, the Business School asked me to come and give one or two lectures, which I did. Then, some time later, they asked me to come back to the school as assistant dean. My office was in University 17 in the room next to where I had met Dean Dunham when he convinced me to stay. I worked in the office with Donald K. David who was also assistant dean. My job was to worry about coordination of courses. I also worked on terminology because, at that time, the terms used in business were not very clear in anybody's mind. I enjoyed that.

I lived at what was then the Colonial Club, with a few very distinguished men, such as Professor Manley Hudson of the Harvard Law

School. I enjoyed living there because outstanding people like Dean Greenough and others in the Department of Economy and the Department of History would come there for lunch or dinner and it also gave me the opportunity to meet officers in different parts of the university. I also presided over meetings of the junior faculty which was very interesting.

Later on, I worked with the architects and my colleagues at the school on the new buildings which were being erected on the other side of the Charles River. One day there were complaints about a gentleman who was teaching factory problems and the dean let him go. The next day he told me to take the course. Well, I didn't know if I could teach or not. At least it was a subject that I felt close to and, while I didn't know very much, I did know a little about it and had studied it very hard. So, I spent hours and hours at night studying and I took a further course in factory problems and systems. I think I had eleven students.

The following year the dean told me to continue teaching and I started a course in Manufacturing, which was then my own course. It was bent toward factory matters, at least at the start. I think I had about ninety or hundred students at that time. I taught in Pierce Hall—PS 110 I think it was called—and then in the Emerson Building. During that period, new buildings were being finished and we moved over. My main recollection is that the dean's office was in Gallatin Hall because Morgan Hall was not finished.

It was during that year that I met Edna Blanche Allen who had just returned from California and was working at the Harvard Economic Service on community services. In California she had been the assistant to the director of the Food Research Institute. Her mother, who had lost her husband, was living in Glendale. Edna became quite interested in the work of the Business School, asked to be transferred to the Business School and became a research assistant.

Also during that period, I had convinced the Chamber of Commerce in Paris to start a school based on the "case system." That school was to be called the C.P.A. Two people from that school, including the director of research, came over to study our methods and decided that we should start, first of all, our own business research centre to be called the Great BRIC. They asked Edna Allen to go over to organize the group of business research and to show them the cases.

Edna met my family in France. By that time I liked her very much and we decided to get married. However, she was not quite convinced that she did not want to go back to California to live. She came back on the French Line, and I went to New York to meet her—Pier 57, North River, New York City. When I arrived at the pier, I realized that two of my competitors for Edna's hand were there also, so I went to the marine superintendent, Tom Wood, a great big, tall, fine Irishman who was a friend of mine. "Tom," I asked, "when the ship docks, who is allowed to go on board?"

He replied, "The French Line personnel, the press, and people with passes, like you." Well, I asked him if on that day he wouldn't mind changing the rule slightly and just let in French Line personnel and the press. He said it was okay with him, and that he would take me in as well. So, when the ship docked I went on board, leaving my two competitors waiting on the dock.

I went to Edna and said, "Look if you don't say that you are going to marry me—I know the French Line very well—you'll stay on that ship, and it will take you back to Paris." So she said that she would marry me. We decided to be married as soon as possible. Edna's mother was older and not well, living in California, and I didn't want my family to take a long, expensive trip to come.

Very intimate friends of ours, Mr. and Mrs. Lewis L. Strauss, offered to have our wedding take place in their home at 25 East 76th Street in New York City. Lewis and Alice Strauss were outstanding people. Lewis was from Virginia, and during the war had taken a job with Herbert Hoover. Later on, he wrote a very interesting book about parts of his life which is called, "Men and Decisions." He did remarkable relief work in Europe under Herbert Hoover. When he returned he joined Kuhn, Loeb & Company leading investment bankers, and shortly became a partner. Alice Strauss was a very intelligent, very kind and able lady whose father was one of the four senior partners of Kuhn Loeb.

I could talk a great deal about Lewis Strauss, but I might simply mention that when World War II came he was called to active duty by the Navy and became a Rear Admiral. Later on, he became chairman of the Atomic Energy Commission. His book tells the story of his life infinitely better than I could. They arranged for the wedding at about 4 o'clock in their attractive house. The minister who married us was the Reverend Minot Simons, a Protestant minister of the Unitarian Church whom I had met in Cleveland.

I might say, in passing, that mother had always written to me to join a church. I investigated Protestant churches and was amazed to find that, in the United States, there must have been tens and tens of different denominations. I could not understand this very easily, because in France if you are a Protestant you either belong to the Reform Church or the Lutheran Church. Fundamentally, it doesn't make much difference and usually depends upon in which part of France you live in. Being from eastern France, I was a Lutheran. One day in Cleveland I was attracted by an electric sign that said First M. E. Church.

The idea of an electric sign on a church was new to me and I came quickly to the unwarranted conclusion that since I had read that there were churches called Christian Scientist probably the sign, First M.E. Church, meant mechanical engineer, which of course proved to be the wrong conclusion. I didn't know what to do until I met the Reverend Minot Simons. I was told that, before becoming a minister, he used to be in the steel business. That sounded very interesting to me and I attended the church in Cleveland. Dr. Minot Simons was a very able and nice person.

Lewis and Alice Strauss organized a small reception. Amongst those who attended the reception were Pierre Cartier of the famous firm of jewelers, Herbert Hoover, Jr., son of the president, and the senior and younger partners of Kuhn Loeb. It was a very happy occasion. The partners of Kuhn Loeb gave us our silverware, glassware, and dinnerware. We spent the evening at the Hotel Weylin.

The next day, our first call as a married couple was on Mr. and Mrs. Jesse Isadore Strauss. Mr. Strauss was then president of NBC and later on became U.S. ambassador to France. We knew them very well and it was a very happy tea at their home. I remember that, when walking on Park Avenue, I would train myself, and looking at imaginary people in the street I would say, "People, please meet Mrs. Doriot." I was training myself to introduce my wonderful wife.

That night we had to go to Cleveland, because I had committed myself to visiting some factories and making a speech. So, our honeymoon was spent in Cleveland. I visited factories, made a speech and didn't spend much time with Edna. We stayed at the home of very fine friends of ours. It was a pleasant time, but not exactly what people believe a honeymoon should be. We came back to Boston, and a few days later I had a call from Kuhn, Loeb and Company telling me that the French Line had asked them for financial help. Kuhn, Loeb wanted to know if I could spend two or three days in Paris and start looking over their situation.

So, Edna and I took a French Line ship, I think it was the *Ile de France* or the *Paris*. The French Line provided us with a very good suite. We arrived in Paris and stayed first with my family, and then came back to the ship pretending we were still on our honeymoon. We were altogether very well taken care of. After that, I left our trunks there, and took only our suitcases on our visits to my family. I worked for three or four days on the ship. It was kind of unconventional, but a lot of fun on a very beautiful ship. Happy and contented, we went back to work at the business school.

We took an apartment in Cambridge. The first Sunday we were

there, everybody in Cambridge seemed to be calling on us. We thought the reason was quite obvious. I had never led any kind of a social life, and practically never went out. I had to work evenings and it appeared that my colleagues wanted to see what Edna was like. And the wives of my colleagues who did not know either me or Edna were also anxious to see what we both looked like. The same thing happened on other evenings. So, after a few weeks we realized that there was no hope of leading any kind of life in Cambridge, and that all my evenings would be wasted and I could not do any work.

So we cancelled the lease and Edna found a home at the Hotel Bellevue in Boston. We decided by that time that we didn't want to live in Cambridge because there would be too much social life with people calling on us without warning. We had a nice little inexpensive home at the Bellevue. During that time Edna started looking for an apartment.

At the Bellevue we did what we could not to spend much money. I remember that we studied the breakfast menus very carefully to see whether we could find a type of breakfast where we would only order for one and would have enough for two. It started to become obvious that tea was preferable to coffee, because with coffee you would usually get one cup, but with tea you would get tea plus hot water so we could have two cups. We also realized that with porridge or things of that type, we could share. One day Edna decided to buy a bigger heater so that we could heat some things, but, unfortunately once I put the heater on the glass top of the table, I proceeded to break the glass, so we didn't end up saving much money.

A short time later, Edna found a very attractive apartment at 5 Arlington Street. It was a three- or four-story house that had been transformed into apartments. We were on the second floor with a balcony overlooking the garden. The rooms, three of them, had high ceilings and were rather attractive. The middle room didn't have any windows, the living room was in front of the garden, the bedroom in the back, and the kitchen on the side. We were really very happy there. At that time there were few automobiles running on Arlington Street and we were not annoyed by their noise or smell.

I don't remember how long we were there, probably a year or year and one-half. Edna met a gentleman who told her that he owned an apartment house at 101 Chestnut Street and he had a very nice duplex apartment on the top two floors which was available. Edna told him that it was too expensive. He said that he very much wanted us to be there and would arrange for the rent to be reasonable. So we took it. We didn't have much furniture but Edna had very good taste. As a matter of fact, I should say extraordinarily good taste, and she managed to pick up furniture here and there. We were very happy in that apartment as well.

After a few years, the lady who had the duplex next door on the same two floors decided she wanted to live elsewhere. She had a long-term lease and couldn't find anyone who wanted the apartment. So she offered to sublet it to us as a very reasonable price. Edna told me that she would like to have it. It had windows on three sides and more space and was really a very beautiful apartment. She said it wouldn't cost us anything to move because all she had to do was push the furniture across the entrance. So, one morning I slept in one apartment and the next morning in the other. We stayed there until the beginning of the war. Of course we knew that once we had to pay the normal rent, we could not keep the apartment.

Edna realized, cheerfully, that she was faced with the problem of finding a place to live. Since I was discussing places to live in, one day she took me to a house on Lime Street which was to be auctioned off. We didn't know how much it would be auctioned for, and I told Edna that the best thing to do would be to watch and if she wanted to, to go to the auction sale. I then left for the Army.

One day Edna called me to say that the house had been auctioned off. In fact, she had gone to the auction and got the house for about eight thousand dollars. That seemed to be a very extravagant price for us to pay for a house that was about my salary at Harvard. But Edna, who always had good, correct feelings about things and about the future, told me that she felt it was decidedly the thing for us to do. We had saved a little money. We did not want to borrow money so we used our savings to buy the house.

Once more, Edna was very clever. She realized that she had to buy some electrical appliances. She had heard that there were two kinds of electric current, DC and AC, and someone told her that the electric current in our district should be changed from DC to AC but they didn't know when. So she went to the Edison Company and told them that we had bought a house and didn't want to buy appliances that would become obsolete; would they please put AC current in our street, at least to our house as soon as possible. Strangely enough, the electric company took her very seriously and gave her AC current. She didn't have to do too much to the house other than fixing up the kitchen. She was about the last one to get stainless steel for the kitchen, which was very fortunate, and helped her make some very simple modifications. It proved to be a very remarkable house and a very remarkable purchase. We have been most happy in that house, and I think our friends have enjoyed it very much. It is a convenient house. The rooms are large and we are on two floors. Our house has twice the width of most of the houses on Lime Street, but of course we had the advantage of only two floors when most of the houses had three or four.

I left Boston and went to Washington D.C. I think it was in June before Pearl Harbor. I lived with friends in the Hotel Carlton. Pearl Harbor came and it was obvious that the war would last long. I called Edna and told her that she had better come to Washington because that is where I was going to be for an undetermined period. I remember that she arrived in Washington one morning on the night train from Boston. She asked me where to look, and for what.

"Well," I said, "we are on Sixteenth Street and it seems to be centrally located. I will be working in the temporary building near the War College. Since it is a long way anyway, I think we should find a place not far from the Carlton. It will be near the shopping district and will be easier for you to go to whatever place you may have to go to."

She said, "All right, I will walk up Sixteenth Street and see what I can find." When I got back to her that night I asked her what happened. She said, "I walked up Sixteenth Street and at Scotts Circle, which is not far from the Carlton, I saw a brand new apartment house. So, I went in. It was not yet occupied, and is available but the apartments are frightfully small." She said that, on the way down in the elevator, she told a very nice black man who ran the elevator her problem and asked him if there wasn't something else there, perhaps like a penthouse. He said, "Yes, madam. There is one penthouse but we are not supposed to tell about it because the owner of the apartment wants to keep it for himself."

Edna always believed that if you don't ask a question, you can't get a yes answer. So she proceeded to go see the owner of the apartment who lived somewhere else, and by evening she had the penthouse. It was very reasonable, very attractive, good air, no noise, and proved to be another very successful decision for Edna. We had two rooms and a nice kitchen and bathroom, and a little concrete space with a fence around it where we could have flowers. The living room is where we lived. In the bedroom we had two beds which we still have in the guest room in Boston. They were along the wall on two sides and in the daytime they looked like sofas. When we invited people to dine with us, we would be in the living room when Edna did the cooking and then we would serve dinner on the bridge table. It worked out very well. We stayed there during the entire war.

I needed people to work for me in Washington. They always had a problem of finding a place to live. It came about that Edna arranged for ten or fifteen of them to live in the same apartment house as we were in, and of course it facilitated the travel problem for us as we could all go to work in the same car.

One event I will always remember about our move to Washington. Edna called me one day and said that she would have dinner with me in our apartment in Washington forty-eight hours later. I asked her how she would do it. Well, she said that the Army told her they would pick up the furniture tomorrow night, ready to be delivered in Washington the next morning, and that I could settle down. Well, I didn't believe that at all. I didn't think the Army could work that fast and that well. But, it was one of the many cases where I underestimated the Army, and also did not realize that the moving was done by the Quartermaster Corps. I belonged to the Quartermaster Corps and, therefore, that made them more efficient. Anyway, she had told me we could have dinner at six o'clock. So, I left the office early. One of my colleagues kept on intruding, making me late. I excused myself saying, "Look, my wonderful wife said I could have dinner at the apartment at six o'clock. There is no possible hope for it, but to go by the house at six o'clock." I went there quite certain that the furniture would not have arrived, but that Edna would be there and the place would be empty. I was mistaken. The furniture had arrived that morning. Edna had arranged everything and had purchased what was necessary and her dinner was ready at six o'clock.

Our life in Washington was very interesting, but in many ways very difficult. When I came there I was told to worry about putting motor transport in production. I was in a room with probably fifty or sixty people. I have a great many papers here in the basement about that phase of the work. Later on, the Quartermaster General told me to worry with conservation because we were short of everything. We had to get the use of aluminum, or copper, or metal of any kind, and it was easier said than done because plastics at that time were really quite unknown as far as their properties are concerned. The knowledge of what they could do was very superficial. Furthermore, since I had to worry about personnel equipment, I discovered people did not realize how important it was to remove from the soldier every possible ounce or fraction of an ounce of excess weight. A man, soldier, must be protected against the weather, he must be able to carry munitions, arms, collective devices, and other essentials. It wasn't easy to find adequate or superior material with light weight. Anyway, we worked at it, and I think fairly successfully.

Later on I was given research and development, including everything connected with the equipment, food, nutrition, and other problems. I have many documents here which explain in detail the work that had to be done. Edna and I got up early and came back to the apartment late. We worked Saturdays and Sundays. My secretary lived in the same apartment building. On Sunday I would tell her that I wasn't going to the office. She had an arrangement with the doorman who would tip her off if I went to the office on Sunday. She would show up there one-half hour later. She was a rather remarkable girl, the daughter of a miner. Her father had become very sick, spending his life mining zinc. At the end of the war I asked her about her overtime payment. She had worked extraordinarily long hours and over weekends. She told me she had not applied for overtime, and I asked her why. She told me that after all it was her contribution to the war effort. Since the girl was really poor, I think that was an admirable viewpoint, and I have seen very little of such devotion.

During that war period Edna also worked very hard. She was manager of the Junior Army-Navy Guild Organization which was called JANGO. It was a volunteer organization taking care of soldiers traveling in and out of Washington or having particular problems in Washington. Mrs. Robert Patterson, wife of a very able undersecretary of war, was the chairman. Edna had to recruit personnel and most of the personnel was made up of children, particularly girls of Army, Navy, Air Force officers and, of course, others. They had canteens and all sorts of organizations. Edna would be up and out most of the day and often during the night. She also worked for another organization.

Later on Mrs. Spats, wife of General Spats of the Air Force, asked her to head up the volunteer money-raising committee for the Washington Symphony Orchestra. She worked very hard at it during the war. She had to do some entertaining, sometimes more than she could handle. We had so many Army people coming to help with our work that very often I had to bring them home for dinner. Quite often I would show up at the house with one or two scientists or industrial people that Edna did not expect, so she had to do whatever she could to get food tickets and buy things in order to be able to feed them.

We had our old Chrysler car which kept on working for a great many years when she needed it for her work and food procurement. Somehow she always managed to have enough gasoline. We were fortunate that she found space in a little garage very close to where we lived, so that made her life easier. We went out very little, and again it was usually with people who had come to help us in the War Department. Fortunately, we were very close to the Statler, Carlton and Mayflower hotels so we could always walk there and it made it very easy, much easier than if we had lived in the suburbs. We never went to a movie or theatre outside once.

Colonel Charles Macarthur was the assistant to the head of chemical warfare, General Porter. He was an extremely pleasant person and I had much to do with him. One day he came into my office and said his wife would be in a play at the theatre on a certain night, here are two tickets, your wife might like to go. I thought it would be nice to take Edna to the theatre and I accepted the tickets and asked the name of the theatre. He looked at me very startled and said, "My, don't you know that there is only one theatre in Washington?" I said that I didn't. To be nice to my colonel friend, I him asked him to come to our apartment after the theatre. It was not far from the theatre and it would be nice to spend a few minutes together.

Well, we went to the theatre and Edna loved it because Helen

Hayes was the leading actress. We went to our apartment and after a few minutes there arrived Colonel Macarthur with his wife Helen Hayes. Of course, neither Edna nor I had connected the name Macarthur with Helen Hayes. It was very exciting, particularly for Edna to have Helen Hayes and her very attractive husband with us for a period of time.

We had the wonderful opportunity of meeting very many outstanding people, particularly from the Army. We received leading British commanders who were research people. I remember that after the war in Europe was over, General Hodges, commander of the First Army, spent his first evening in Washington having a little dinner at Scotts Circle with us. All those gentlemen were very outstanding and, in a way, amongst them I felt there was a higher ratio of devoted, able people than one usually meets in business. I am happy to say that I have a great many photographs of them and also letters. I kept in close touch with the Army Corps and Division Commanders about their equipment. After all, they were my clients and I wanted to please them, and by doing our job well we were saving lives.

I had the great opportunity to see General Marshall several times. Someday I will write stories or anecdotes about some of the things that he told me. So, I would say that our stay in Washington was a most interesting one. Of course, there were things I had to worry about because mistakes were costly, not only in terms of life, but also in terms of precise dates to be met for certain operations. After the war was over, Secretary Patterson called me and told me that the Army was going to form G-5 on The First Venture Capitalist's staff and that it would be a new department for research and development. He said that General Eisenhower and he were of the opinion that I should be asked to take charge of the department.

I told him that I couldn't accept because I had to go back to Harvard or somewhere and start earning my living again. Since I had very few years of service, my Army pay wasn't very high and I just had to work.

While we could live on my salary, we could not save on it. Well, the secretary said they were going to ask somebody else to take it, but because of my experience would I be willing to go in for a period of months as his deputy. I said I would do that.

The person they were going to ask was General Dolittle. One day General Dolittle, whom I had known, came into my office all excited and said, "Look, they want me to come back and take that job. But nobody tells Jimmy what to do." He said that if he was told he had to take it, he probably would, but they had started the conversation by saying "Jimmy you probably don't want it." So, he said, "What the hell, I am not taking it."

Eventually, they chose an officer who, to my mind, was not at all the right man. He had had a very ordinary career but he was regular Army. At that time he was at Walter Reed trying to get himself out of the Army for disability. I stayed on the job for several months and did not particularly enjoy it. There was no hope of doing anything very constructive and everybody was sort of bossed out and fed up with Army expenditures. In the meantime, however, I should say that the secretary of the Treasury, Mr. Snyder, had called and told me that he had one very big problem which was the disposal of surplus—Army, Navy, and Air Force surplus of all types. They had an organization going and I think it was under Mr. Stuart Symington, who later went on to become secretary of the Air Force and a senator.

Mr. Snyder told me that they were going to merge all the activities on surplus into a single organization called War Assets Administration and said that he had come to the conclusion that I should take it. I gave him the same answer that I had previously given, that I had to go back to earn my living. Well, Mr. Snyder asked me if I would pick someone to head it up. I told him that the ideal man was Lieutenant-General Edmund Gregory who had been quite a successful and outstanding Quartermaster General since before the war and is still there now. So he said that they would ask General Gregory and would I go in as his deputy. I told him that the Army had just asked me to go on the general's staff for a while. Well he said that he would arrange things with the Army and that the Army could wait, but War Assets couldn't.

General Gregory was made head of War Assets and I went in as a deputy. I then left the Quartermaster Corps. Work was interesting; it was also bewildering. I had more friends than I could cope with. Governors and presidents of companies would come looking for something to be purchased at a low cost. It was a huge organization with surplus all over the world. I inherited about fourteen divisions, most of them were people that were or were not suited for the job.

I had one very special experience which I can't recount here, but I have notes in my files. It was very interesting and very peculiar, but I suppose I should not talk about it. Anyway, that lasted for three or four months. I tried to get an organization going. By that time General Gregory had developed some physical trouble and resigned. He was replaced by someone of very different distinction. The only story I might tell about that is that, later on, we found that people were offered jobs without the organization knowing who they were. It was one of the worst cases of distributing jobs to please politicians. I even understand that there were records showing that people who had died were still being offered jobs.

I might tell one amusing story about that. One day a senator called me and said he was on the committee supervising us and wanted to come and ask me about a plan. He came and I told him what our plans were, and I remember mentioning to him that there would be an announcement the next day. I stressed that it was confidential until announced. But that very afternoon the newspapers in Washington came out with a statement by the senator saying that Senator So and So demands that War Assets tell us as follows. This confirms the idea that I had formed during the war that you could find outstanding senators in Washington and also some others who were quite different.

We will perhaps never know the "special experience" that Georges Doriot stopped short of recounting. It is not difficult to observe, given his proximity to people of power, that he was probably privy to many special experiences. A few days later, on April 24, 1980, Georges continued with his story. On this occasion, he would share with us his unostentatious dreams, his boundless faith in and love for his wife Edna, and his deep appreciation of hard-working men, and his distaste for duplicity and deception.

Sometime before 1914, father and mother had built a very nice little house in one of the western suburbs of Paris right after you have crossed the River Seine. The area occupied a high ground above the Seine. It is on the main line railroad station and, at the present time, it is only six minutes from Paris by electric train.

At that time, it was mostly populated by people of medium to modest means and many foreigners, mostly English or Dutch, who worked in Paris. The family bought a little plot of land and erected a most attractive, very convenient house which they designed themselves. Over the years, it has proved to be a very good place to live. After father died, mother stayed there, and after mother died, my sister and her husband, who was the Lutheran minister for that particular parish, came to live at 7 Rue Franklin and are still there.

Some time after World War II when Edna and I were there, one Sunday I helped a little in the garden, which is very small but very attractive, and I casually remarked to Edna that someday we might have a little garden of our own. She didn't say anything.

We had never lived in the suburbs and didn't want to. We were then living in Boston. So, when we talked about a garden it meant, to Edna, that perhaps we should have a little place in the country. I didn't pay too much attention to my remark, but several months later Edna told me that she had been looking around with her sister, Nell, for a little place in the country. They didn't know whether to look on the North Shore, South Shore or west of Boston. Somehow Edna, instinctively, made up her mind that the North Shore would be better. It was close to Boston and she knew that if we had a place a long distance from Boston, we would never go there. So, one day she told me that she had found a plot of land in Manchester, Massachusetts, and she wanted me to go and see it.

I went to see it with her. It was very nice, about one and three-quarter acres right above water on large rocks. It was owned by the widow of a gentleman who came from Worcester from a well-known Worcester family. On that plot of land had stood a house which, I believe, was called Cragside. It was a four-story house, quite large. As a matter of fact, I should say very large, and it had a tower over it. After the gentleman died, his widow bulldozed it down, because the house was quite large and the taxes were very high. Much of the rubble had been taken out, but there was still a substantial amount still there. What we were really doing was buying a large plot of land with much rubble. In Manchester, there is a book on my shelves which shows a picture of that house.

When I went to look at it again, Edna and I thought that we should buy a little more land so as to protect ourselves from neighbors being too close or building too close to us. A friend of ours, Mr. Pope, had purchased land next to us from the same estate. So, we talked to him about it. He was a very kind and friendly person, and sold back to us what I would think was probably another acre, so we had close to three acres. The garden was in terrible shape. Nature had taken it over. The local expert on gardening told Edna that there was no hope for the garden and it would be too expensive to fix. Edna, as I discovered later, didn't pay any attention to that.

We finally bought the house from the estate. I think the name of the lady we bought it from was a Mrs. Stackpole. Before the purchase, one day Edna asked Mr. Mel Griswold, our good friend, to go and see that land with us. When we arrived there, we found that a friend of theirs, the president of a well-known company in Boston, was looking the land over with his wife. Edna, always frank and outgoing said, "Look, if you want it, I won't even try to get it." "Oh no," said the friend, "We really have no interest in it."

After they left, Edna told me that she had a strange feeling that the people did not tell Mel and herself their exact feeling, and Edna felt that they really wanted that land. Edna suggested to Mel that we go to the real-estate agent immediately. We went to the agent's office and found, indeed, those people had just told him that they wanted the land. That was, what you might call, an interesting situation.

Mel Griswold was very mad that his particular friend had said that he was not interested and then almost immediately tried to get it. Mel helped Edna convince the Stackpole estate that she was the one who should get it. Mrs. Stackpole, or her lawyers, I don't quite remember who, felt the same way as Mel Griswold and we got the land. It is interesting to remember that Edna had had a similar problem when she purchased the house at 12 Lime Street. She felt that she had almost been double crossed by the real estate man, and went to the Real Estate Board who told her she was right, and that the particular agent had not behaved as he should have.

Anyway, we got the land and decided to purchase a little Walpole tool house. It was a nice, attractive, tiny wood structure and was very inexpensive. It had a bedroom, a tiny living room, kitchen and bath, about sixty or eighty square feet. Later on, we added a porch. While it was an attractive little thing, it was unprotected against heat and cold. There was no heat in it, and in the summer it was extremely hot. We lived there about twenty years and we still have it. It was a very happy little love nest, and while it wasn't too comfortable, Edna, helped by Eda (Doriots' European housekeeper) would very often invite eight or ten people and we would have a nice dinner.

During that period, Edna and Eda went to work very hard to clean up the garden. They fixed up one place with ropes and pulleys, and one day I found them lifting piles of boulders and stones from a great big hole near the house, lifting them over the wall with the pulleys and ropes and then using a wheelbarrow to take them out. They worked extremely hard. Then they built the steps. I have a copy of a letter from Edna to the Boston and Maine Railroad saying, "Dear Sir, I have seen some old railroad ties which are piled up unused, could I have them?" They said yes and Edna went to get them. They sawed them in half, and one can still see many steps in the garden made from those ties.

We decided to put a fence around the place because our land was used by all sorts of people for picnicking. Whenever we would go there, we would find broken bottles. Much damage was done by children of neighbors. We had a very nice vine producing good grapes. The fruit would all disappear. We also had beautiful flagstones and those flag-stones disappeared. We had walls and the walls disappeared, or at least the stones disappeared. It was very bad. Therefore, we put up an attrac-tive Walpole fence. The neighbors objected, but we said that we were very sorry, but that was the only way we could protect our place. We had ivy and a few months later it had all been pulled out. So indeed, we needed a fence.

Inside of our fenced lot we lived happily. Edna would go there during the week with the car. I would take the train and she would meet me, smilingly, at the station. And since nobody really knew we were there, we didn't have any kind of social life. I remember that during all those years we perhaps went out once to a particularly close friend's house. We enjoyed the seclusion. As a matter of fact, many years later the police were very much surprised to learn that there was anyone living at the place.

Well, during that period, Edna kept on dreaming about someday erecting a very nice house. We didn't have money to spend on it, so we saved. We talked to different architects, and after twenty-five or twenty-seven years Edna finally had a set of plans that she liked and an architect who was very imaginative and artistic, and understood Edna's expectations. We wanted a single house, very simple and reliable, well protected against fire and other such happenings, with easy upkeep and maintenance. We wanted it to blend into the rocks so that it would look simple and modest, and I think that Edna's dreams were realized. The house is attractive, simple, and extremely easy for upkeep and maintenance.

When the house was almost finished, Edna realized that behind the house we still had old walls that could be used, and she suggested to the architect that we turn that space into a guest house. It was done, and the guest house is most attractive. Many of the old walls were used, as many as we could, but we did have to tear down some of them. Well, thinking back about my remark made in France, Edna had acted on it as she always did. One day when the house was built she said, "You had said once that you would like to have a little land somewhere to plant a garden," and she laughed and said, "We now have it." That is the story of Manchester.

Manchester has proven to be very wonderful. It is a nice village. We are in what is called "Smith's Point" which is about a mile and one-half away from the village. We have an absolutely perfect view. The house faces south. On the left hand we can see the eastern-point lighthouse in Gloucester, and on the right hand side we see trees from Smith's Point. The water is right below us and it really is a very marvelous view. While we have had some winter damage, we don't get too much of it. It has never been a great catastrophe, but we do have to protect the house against salt air. A year ago we had the walls sprayed with silicone. It is an easy house to live in and is really most attractive, with much sunlight. All the windows facing south are very large, and we have been there in the winter when it was below freezing. During the daytime, if there is sun, the temperature in those rooms was around seventy degrees and did not need electric heating.

We were amazed at the very high taxes. When the house was built, we were really overtaxed and were very much put out. I told the tax people that in the south, the city would have given us a break on taxes. I said that it was the only new house built, we were aged, we were not going to live for too many years, and we were making a present to the city of an income-earning property. Well, after a year and a half, the city had some outsiders make some evaluation again, and our taxes were decreased, but they are still very high. The house is completely heated by electricity, which we felt was wise.

When Edna was planning the house, the electric company explained to us that we would get special rates because we were all electric. Of course, that didn't prove to be a true statement. When the energy crisis came, our electric bill was fairly high. We had very good people building the house. The only bad one was a local electrician. He was lazy and I don't think he knew what he was doing. Everybody in the city advised us to take him. They told us he was the city electrician, and therefore he was very good. He proved to be quite worthless, and even now we still have problems because of poor connections. In some cases, the connections were never made. I understand that he has left Manchester and is now living in Gloucester. I would suggest that no one who lives in our house in years to come use him again.

The other people who worked there were very good, particularly Frank Mogavero, an Italian-born master mason living in Revere. Most of his workers were Italian born. They were very artistic, as one can see to this day by looking at the stone walls inside and outside the house. They worked very hard and were very devoted to Edna. We really enjoyed them very much. We are pleased to say very nice things about them. Mogavero has proven to be a very good friend and a skillful person. Edna did not know much Italian, but she enjoyed practicing it with these people, and so did Eda. Mogavero always remains at our disposal for anything that we need whether at the house in Manchester or at the house in Boston. He has a very wonderful Italian wife and very attractive, well-brought-up children. It was a pleasure, and it still is a pleasure to have him around.

Edna used very little help for her garden. As a matter of fact, Eda resents anybody who comes to help. Even working on the slope going toward the water, Eda would rather rope herself on a tree and go down the rope to fix things than have someone come and do it. The garden is not what one might call a fine garden, but it is very beautiful. Edna helped a great deal in the garden, but fundamentally the garden is Eda's creation.

Eda is quite sold on Manchester. It really is her farm. Since she was brought up as one of about fifteen children in Fritogen in the Bernese Alps, she loves Manchester and would much prefer to be there than here. Of course, at the present time, it is not as pleasant for her. When she had Edna, they would walk through the garden, make plans, deciding which flowers went where and why, and that made Eda's life much more interesting than it now is. While I do appreciate what she does, I don't have the ability, knowledge or the good taste to discuss what should be done. I don't know anything else to say about Manchester outside of the fact that it was a wonderfully constructive step in my life.

Edna died in 1978, and while he carefully guarded his sense of loss, Georges Doriot made no secret of the memories of which she remained an inviolable part.

THE BIRTHDAY PARTY

RALPH JOHN SODA

(In the 1980s, journalist and author Ralph Soda was commissioned to write a book on General Doriot. For a variety of reasons the book was never completed. But Soda's description of the 80th birthday party for Doriot seems more than a fitting ending to The First Venture Capitalist.*)*

IT WAS A GATHERING OF GIANTS to honor a Titan. More than 450 of the most-powerful business leaders from two continents converged on Harvard's Burden Hall in Boston that bright autumnal day. It was September 24, 1979. It was his birthday. And they had come to salute the General. Gen. Georges F. Doriot, professor emeritus of the Harvard Business School—teacher, soldier, painter, poet, entrepreneur and lover. It was an event the staid Harvard Business School Bulletin would later proclaim was "... so far as is known, unique in the history of the School." That comment is not surprising. Almost everything about Doriot was unique. For 40 years his famed second-year course, titled merely Manufacturing was the most popular of the Business School's curriculum; Doriot, its most sought-after teacher. By the time he retired in 1966, he had taught more than 7,000 students—three generations of American businessmen—and he was revered by reputation in corporate boardrooms and college lecture halls throughout the world. Such a career would be accomplishment enough for most in a lifetime. For Doriot, it was just one in a parade of outstanding achievements, some of them already legend.

Doriot founded the venture-capital industry in the United States, Canada, and Europe, launching more than 200 companies—Digital Equipment Company among them. The Institut Europeen d'Administration des Affairs (INSEAD), which is today Europe's leading graduate school of business, owes its establishment to Doriot's genius. He also helped create the U.S. Army Industrial College. And he made a hero's contribution to the Allied Cause in World War II, when as a brigadier general in the War Department—he pioneered the research and led the effort that succeeded in making America's GI Joe the best-equipped fighting man ever to take the field of battle in the world's long history of war. General Doriot was awarded the U.S. Distinguished Service Medal; decorated a commander of the British Empire and of France's Legion of Honor, received honorary degrees from six colleges and universities, and was a member of the American Academy of Arts and Sciences. And there are the testimonials:

- 1966, Business Statesman of the Year, Harvard Business School Club of New York City.

- 1973, Distinguished Citizens Award HBS Club of New York City.

- 1974, Distinguished Service Award, Harvard Business School Association.

- 1979, National Business Hall of Fame, Fortune Magazine.

But now that all seemed such a long time ago. Already it was 1979, and the year had slipped unnoticed into its final quarter. Soon it too would be over. And ahead crouched another long twelve months of emptiness. Edna had been dead for a year now. And with her, so much of himself had died. How was it possible even to imagine life without his Edna, let alone to go on living it? She had been his loving wife and dearest friend for more than 48 years. And—praise him as they might—Doriot knew that whatever inspiration, whatever good he may have given others in his lifetime had come to him first through Edna. Now she was gone, leaving him with a sudden, secret dread that the world too might know that now—alone—he had nothing else to give. He was—as in the title of the Robert Frost poem—BEREFT. Since Edna's death, Doriot had saved several copies of the final stanza of that poem among his papers at 12 Lime Street in Boston and at their cliff-top, oceanfront retreat, just up the coast in Manchester, Massachusetts BEREFT. It explained it all so well and the words came back to him now, amid the cheery din of Burden Hall.

> Leaves got up in a coil and hissed.
> Blindly struck at my knees and missed.
> Something sinister in the tone.
> Told me my secret must be known:
> Word I was in the home alone
> Somehow must have gotten abroad.
> Word I was in my life alone,
> Word I had no one left but God.

Alone, and yet surrounded by a crowd. Doriot grimaced at the thought, and straightened his shoulders in an effort to shake free of his dreary mood. Edna would never approve such gloomy introspection. No. Not at all. She would expect him to be strong—like he used to pretend he was to her—to welcome the guests and thank them for their generosity, on her behalf as well. For this birthday celebration was also a tribute to Edna's memory, in that it also doubled as a benefit fundraiser for The French Library in Boston of which Edna had been president. That was the main reason he was here. An acutely private person, Georges Doriot instinctually recoiled from ostentation of any kind. Public testimonials, of which he was the focus, particularly embarrassed him. If given the chance, he would refuse them. But a benefit for The French Library in Boston? Ah, that was something else again. Yes, he would do that, he told members of the birthday celebration committee. He would do it for Edna.

The library was conceived near the end of World War II when a group of Free French supporters "rescued" 500 French books, which the Vichy government had cached in a Boston warehouse. Since then, development of the library into the major cultural center it eventually became was one of Edna Doriot's lifetime passions. Edna drove herself tirelessly on behalf of the library, first as an ordinary, stamp-licking volunteer and later as president. Progress was slow, but steady.

The library flourished. And forty years later, largely because of Edna Doriot's leadership, The French Library in Boston could boast of 40,000 volumes, and a respectable collection of films and tapes. She lived to see it eventually acclaimed one of the leading institutions in this country dedicated to French-American relationships. For their efforts in this direction, Edna and Georges Doriot were inducted Commanders in the French Legion of Honor, one of the few couples in history ever so honored. But then in 1976, it began to unravel.

Edna was stricken with lymphoma. Her sickness became his preoccupation. For a while, it seemed she would recover. But it was only for a while. When finally forced to face up to the cruel reality of the disease that was gnawing away at her vitality, the General gave Edna his promise. Whatever happened, she was not to worry: he would carry on her work for the Library. And that resolve, too, he preserved in lines from a Thomas Gray poem—multiple copies of which were also filed away among his papers. It so beautifully expressed Edna's desire.

> If I should die and leave you here awhile,
> Be not like others, soon undone, who keep

Long vigil by the silent dust and weep.
For my sake turn again to life and smile,
Nerving thy heart and trembling hand to do
Something to comfort weaker hearts than thine.
Complete those dear unfinished tasks of mine,
And, I, perchance, may therein comfort you.

So—nerving his heart—Doriot edged into the well of Burden Hall, with Edna on his arm. He stretched on tiptoe, straining to see over heads in the crowd in a vain attempt to get a sense of their number. And then he looked up at the tier upon tier of rising row of seats, stacked amphitheater style—like bleachers in a bandstand—climbing to the ceiling. There were so many people.

More than 450 of them, he was told. Former students mostly. The rest, friends, business associates, and their friends. He was touched by their presence. He later admitted to feeling a little proud.

"I've often said that my only interest in teaching is that I hope that five years after you've read or heard what I have to say, you'll respect me," he would tell his classes. "I've always said I have a choice—either you'll like me now or you'll respect me in five or six years. And by experience and for my own conscience, I like the second better."

There could be little doubt. Doriot's conscience was at peace. And he was smiling. He might have had in mind the Marcus Aurelius quote he found in one of Edna's diaries after she died.

I affirm that tranquility is nothing else than a good ordering of the mind.

Yes, the General had taught his students well. And they had not forgotten. His wisdom had become their good fortune. He was the genius of their success. So they had come back, to show their gratitude and to thrill to the magic one more time. Now the professor moved among them once again, fluidly—a tall, gaunt, erect, eighty-year-old, with a quiet manner and an elegant bearing that invited confidence and discourages familiarity, both at the same time.

It is a part of the Doriot signature, that elegant manner. That and his rich French accent.

You never forgot the accent. It was so distinctive, throaty almost but with a velvet purr. And you can hear it now—even in the happy hubbub of this crowded lecture hall—as Doriot works the room, greeting his former pupils individually and by name; acknowledging their presence with a tight, Gaelic bow; his kind, blue eyes brightening Eagle-like with merry attention, as each new recognition evokes old recollections. Many of those present were business colleagues of his, as well as former students. It is understandable, given the fact that Doriot had, at varying times in his career, been a director of sixteen companies, and that many of his students had gone on to be employed by the more than 200 businesses and industries which owed their existences to his venture-capital trailblazing.

The membership list of the birthday celebration committee alone reads like a blue book of corporate royalty. Among them; Robert A. McCabe of New York, then a partner in Lehman Brothers, Kuhn Loeb and later founder of Pilot Capital Corporation; Sanford C. Bernstein, president of the Wall Street investment firm of Sanford C. Bernstein Company, Inc.; Kenneth Olsen, chairman of Digital Equipment Corp.; Walter A. Haas, Jr., chairman of Levi, Strauss & Company.; Philip Caldwell, president of the Ford Motor Company; James D. Robinson 3d, chairman of American Express; Dorothy Rowe, first treasurer of Digital Equipment Company, Claude Janssen of Europe's Banque Worms; prominent French businessmen, Arnaud de Vitry and Aynmar de Lastours of France and John S.R. Shad, chairman of the Securities and Exchange Commission. Some of those present he hadn't seen in years, but most of that group could be counted as part of the procession that, down through the decades, had visited him and Edna at their home at 12 Lime Street. In his moving eulogy—To Georges F.

Doriot from a Friend—written after the General's death on June 2, 1987, Robert McCabe recalled those visits.

> Even after he became ill they kept coming for advice on business and personal matters. The General's approach was usually not to lecture, but rather to ask a very few penetrating questions. Usually the advice seeker would leave, having answered his own questions.

Remarkably few among the 450 at the General's birthday celebration did not know the General well. Many had kept in regular correspondence with him since leaving Harvard years before. Others he saw regularly at business or social functions. They were close friends. A few—McCabe, Kenneth Olsen, Arnaud de Vitry; his lawyer, Richard Testa, and Dorothy Rowe—were practically family. Especially Dorothy Rowe.

Those few were the regulars at the memorable New Year's Eve dinner parties, which had become a tradition at the Doriots. They were the summer guests at Manchester, the "Bidders," for whom the General would delight in holding mock "auctions" of his paintings—gem-like, floral still lifes of delightful, dazzling color, which at Edna's suggestion he had taken to doing for relaxation, according to McCabe;

> General Doriot's paintings were all done on 7" x 10" canvases, with a palette knife, The size of the canvas never varied, notwithstanding gifts of larger canvases and the entreaties of friends. He would explain that the time he had available for painting coupled with the high cost of pigments dictated the size.
>
> He gave many of his paintings away to friends and occasionally would "auction" them to friends with thirty-nine cents being the maximum selling price. The General sometimes mentioned that two of his paintings were in the Metropolitan Museum in New York—one in the office of a former student, the other in storage as part of the collection of the late Robert Lehman. Several years ago, Harvard's Fogg Art Museum used one of his paintings in a calendar.

General and Mrs. Doriot for many years gave black-tie New Year's Eve parties at their home at 12 Lime Street in Boston's Beacon Hill section. Every year after dinner, he would give a humorous talk on some topical theme. One was particularly memorable. He complained that his status as a naturalized U.S. citizen precluded his becoming president of the United States and that that was unfair, so he had tried to think of other ways to achieve power and influence. He finally, he said, thought of a way to become more powerful than the president: he would start and head a union of computer programmers. That would give power over banks, insurance companies, and the government itself.

The General had a close inner circle. None was closer than Dorothy Rowe. It was Dorothy who inherited most of those exquisite, palette-knife paintings left behind at his death. She had been his associate since the end of World War II when—together with Karl T. Compton, head of Massachusetts Institute of Technology, former New Hampshire Senator Ralph Flanders and other visionaries wanting to continue the technological lead gained by American industry in the war years—Doriot founded The American Research and Development Corporation, and launched the venture-capital industry in America. Dorothy was his administrative assistant at ARD, rising to senior vice president and treasurer.

When Doriot advanced $70,000 to a young MIT engineer by the name of Kenneth Olsen to start a computer company, Dorothy Rowe became the first treasurer of Digital Equipment Company, the phenomenal success that Olsen's dream and Doriot's confidence helped spawn.

And later, when Doriot was being pressured to sell his stock in Digital, it was Dorothy Rowe who persuaded him to hold on. He did. And at the time of his death, newspaper accounts placed the value of his DEC stock at near $50 million. Rowe's career looms even more remarkable, when one considers the period during which it flourished. It was put in perspective on May 12, 1985, when she was awarded the honorary degree of Doctor of Laws by Emerson College. The commemoration read in part: "In those male-dominated days prior to the 'Women's Movement,' you and a handful of other women were movers and shakers in corporate territory that was a professional mine field to members of your sex."

Is it any wonder then, that this former WAVES lieutenant, who served with distinction in the Navy Gunnery and Bombsight Officers School during World War II, should in time become Gen. Doriot's closest confidantes? It was no secret that Doriot valued her counsel and respected her skills as much as he did any man's, if not more. He provided tangible evidence of that esteem later, awarding her an honorary diploma as a graduate of his course in Manufacturing. It is a distinction shared only by one other person—another esteemed friend: Robert A. McCabe.

When Edna died, it was Dorothy who emerged as the principal source of comfort in his loneliness. She was available whenever he needed her, now the discreet adviser, now the indispensable Girl Friday. She accompanied him on business trips and helped plan his social calendar. They became almost constant dinner companions, at 12 Lime Street and on rare evenings out.

For his part, Doriot openly fretted over Dorothy's stubbornly incessant smoking and her worsening emphysema. He would telephone her every night before retiring to satisfy himself she had arrived safely back home to her townhouse, around the corner on Charles Street. And lately, he found himself more and more troubled by the restless moods of nervous desperation, which, accompanied by fits of anorexia, stalked her with ever-increasing frequency.

Probably only Dorothy Rowe knew the real reason for her anxiety. But Dorothy confided in no one on matters of such a personal nature, least of all in Doriot. And, yet, it was obvious to anyone who cared enough to see. Dorothy Rowe was sad. It wasn't easy having to stand by helplessly, while her once invincible General fought a lonely, losing battle with the demons of his own decline—Edna's death, advancing age, and an ominously frequent, wracking cough. Nor does it matter that the hero dies bravely. The nobler the death, the more poignant the sorrow. Dorothy was often desolate at the prospect of tomorrow.

But she hid it well. It is doubtful Doriot ever realized the extent of her concern for him. And it's a mark of her own courage and selflessness that she was able to shield him from the source of her distress. She thought it was for his sake that she had done so. And who could say she was wrong? Except for Edna, no one knew Georges Doriot better than Dorothy Rowe. And that, he did know.

He was comfortable with her. They shared many of the same views on politics, business, and religion. It was uncanny the way she could anticipate his moods and sense his feelings. There were occasions when she would predict his reaction to a particular situation, before he himself even had a hint of how he might respond. The fact is, very little happened with Georges Doriot these days that Dorothy Rowe wasn't a part of. She had, for example, played a key role in the planning of this: his 80th birthday celebration. Throughout the afternoon, he glimpsed her fluttering among the guests, putting her final worrying touches on its organization. And he could feel her watching him now—as she was given to doing in unguarded moments—with the wary gaze of a mother cat, spying from a distance on her kittens at play.

Burden Hall was abuzz with excitement. Everyone was talking at once. The efforts of committee members to get everyone seated and the program started on time went unheeded. Guests were still arriving; the confusion was building. And then—just when it seemed sure everything would disintegrate in chaos—order took hold. Gradually the seats filled up. When there were no more available, they sat in the aisles—more than 450 distinguished men and fashionably dressed women, struggling to restrain their noisy gaiety, squeezing in together wherever space allowed—like children at a sold-out matinee. And then Doriot moved to the lectern, and a hush fell over the room.

Something special was on the agenda that day. Anticipation was everywhere. Doriot—the engraved invitations proclaimed with heraldic pomp and promise—was going to give an encore. It was true. The General had agreed to break a thirteen-year, self-imposed classroom silence—resulting from his retirement—and teach a one-time refresher class in Manufacturing. It would be his gift to them on his birthday.

McCabe and Bernstein, co-chairmen of the event, were ecstatic. A refresher in Manufacturing would be the highlight of the program. For as Doriot was unique among college professors, Manufacturing was unique among graduate-school business courses. To start with, the title Manufacturing, was deceptively modest for a course so ambitious. It came close to being a misnomer. Doriot taught a way of life, as opposed to a vocational discipline. And his course, Manufacturing, in truth, had more to do with the making of men than the making of the products men make.

Almost without exception, those students fortunate enough to have taken it remember the class as one of the more exciting and rewarding experiences of their learning years, and Doriot, as an educator without peer. To *Forbes* magazine, Doriot was "A Teacher Who Made A Difference." To Philip Caldwell, former chairman of the Ford Motor Company, he was the inspiration that enabled Caldwell to arrest Ford's recent slide into mediocrity and to return the company to its once pre-eminent position in the forefront of the American automotive industry. Caldwell still remembers the Doriot maxim that was part of that inspiration.

Gentlemen, if you want to succeed in business, you must love your product.

"He taught me how to think. More importantly, he taught me to think. The things he taught me are more important thirty-five years out of school than they were when I began my career," Caldwell said.

"By any measure, you'd have to say that General Doriot was one of the greatest of teachers."

Digital's Kenneth Olsen agrees. Speaking at Doriot's eightieth-birthday celebration, he praised The First Venture Capitalist's contributions to DEC. "He is in greater demand by my people than ever before. He is more pertinent with his comments than ever before. I told him to come pack in ten years and we'll talk about his retirement." And Olsen was true to his word. It is a tribute to Doriot that up until his death at the age of 87, The General remained an active DEC director. When he became too ill to leave the house, the DEC board of directors met at 12 Lime Street.

In an interview with *The Economist*, Olsen described Doriot's influence on DEC as "quiet, cautious, often indirect . . . his thinking and Digital's history and values are intertwined." According to *The Economist*: "That thinking persuaded Mr. Olsen to institute day-care centers and maternity leave for employees, helping to make DEC one of the most progressive employers in America." DEC also became one of the most successful businesses in America.

"I flowered under him," William McGowan, founder and chairman of MCI, says of Doriot. And James D. Robinson III, chairman of Shearson-American Express said: "Doriot taught the commitment and the sense of responsibility needed to succeed in business. These were conveyed either directly or indirectly by his own actions. He was one of the most interesting men I have ever met." Gen. Doriot had also taught Robinson's father, and it was a point of personal pride to him that he helped educate three generations of America's leading businessmen. But the Doriot legend is more than that. He had vision. He was the first to anticipate the decline of U.S. Steel—and that from just a brief glimpse of its management style. Perhaps his finest contribution to both his students and his era remains his tireless insistence on the need for high ethical and moral standards—standards without which business success as measured in profit becomes merely greed. "Long before

business ethics became an issue, Doriot was emphasizing the importance of character, integrity, and common sense in his famous course on
Manufacturing, *The Economist* reported on the occasion of his death.

The Harvard Business School Bulletin aptly summed up the impact of
the teacher on his students:

> They, for the most part, remember well what he's said and what he
> stands for; they carry with them the effects of his demanding require-
> ments of dress and behavior, 19 of ethical conduct, of intellectual chal-
> lenge, and of a sense of the future. They recall his influence on their own
> careers. The excitement of his classes remains clear in memory.

But that came after. In the beginning, there were times during the
school year for the students Manufacturing seemed just plain, punish-
ing drudgery. Doriot believed in hard work. "We should give beauty to
the word 'work,'" he would say. "Leisure is a fake." Doriot students
kept rigorous schedules. They were expected to labor as unpaid consultants with actual companies. They learned management problem-
solving by solving real-life management problems.

"He believed you would learn best by being involved in a business,"
McGowan recalls. But that was only part of it. At the same time, the
students were required to devote a full year to researching and reporting on developments vital to business, both in the present and in the
future. The papers resulting from this research were the famed "topic
reports" of Doriot legend. "Many of these 'topic reports' were eventually published, placing their authors on the leading edge of important
new trends and technologies," the *HBS Bulletin* reported.

One of the best-known examples is the "topic report" that management consultant John Diebold did for Doriot in 1950. That research
report spawned the word "automation," and Diebold used it as the
basis for his first book, *Automation, The Advent of the Automatic Factory*
(Van Nostrand, 1952). It came about when Doriot suggested Diebold

interview some of the greatest thinkers of the day, as part of his topic report project—thinkers like the mathematics genius, John von Neumann. Thirty years later, Diebold relived that assignment in an interview for *Computerworld* magazine.

> I had been doing a paper for General Doriot, and he suggested people I should see as part of my research—John von Neumann, Norbert Wiener and others. So I had written to von Neumann and asked if I could come to Princeton and see him during Christmas vacation time.
>
> I remember it very dramatically. The snow had just fallen, an absolutely perfect cover of snow on the long tree-lined entrance coming to the Institute for Advanced Studies. And from von Neumann's office, I could see a figure trudging in the snow. An almost surrealistic scene— his lone figure in the unbroken snow. As the figure got closer, I realized it was Albert Einstein! If only I had had a camera. In the session with von Neumann, I asked, 'Could you use automatic control devices and computers for factory control?' I outlined the sort of thing we were interested in, having a computer overerride control and coordination on all factory operations. He went to a blackboard and wrote some equations, describing things that were far beyond my understanding of mathematics. He would pause occasionally and ask. 'Isn't this right?' or 'Isn't that right?' —I mean, here was the greatest mathematician in the world asking me if he was right!
>
> After a while, he said computers would be able to do that and, yes, as computers developed, theoretically the whole thing should work. And I said, "What are you going to do about that?" And he said, "I'm not going to do anything about that—you go and do something about it! I'm happy knowing it can be done. I deal in theory. You go deal with the problem of making it happen.

Diebold's groundbreaking was not unique in the course in Manufacturing. On the contrary. Again, according to the *Harvard Business School Bulletin,*

> . . . as early as 1951, for example, some "Doriot men" were looking closely at the uses of lasers.

That was the kind of innovation Doriot craved in his students. He exhilarated in the uncommon, the bold, and the venturesome. He treasured individuality over mass standardization and he had little patience with the regimented banality of established institutions—whether corporate America, or revered academia. Not even Harvard Business School was spared.

> For years I have objected to "résumés"—soon an IBM card. Is that a description or evaluation of an individual? Young people already think of themselves as an IBM card. The résumé is to my mind a symbol of modern stupidity. Still great big business schools, etc., worship the résumés. It is standardization to the extreme of narrow-mindedness.

Nor did Doriot have much patience with those merely skilled at the manipulation of numbers. Though trained as an accountant—or maybe because of it—he was suspicious of the "bean counter" mentality. So far as Doriot was concerned, juggling was a dexterity best left to the circus. To succeed in business—to really succeed—one needed integrity, performance, and an awareness of reality.

Doriot expressed these criteria in a series of stiletto-sharp maxims, which he drove home to his students with a fierce, narrow-eyed intensity calculated to underscore their importance.

> Success with modesty, oblivion if we can learn from it.
> Gentlemen, if you want to be a success in business, you must love your product.
> Sell it, or make it. Don't track it.
> Remember, somebody, somewhere is designing a product that will make your product obsolete.

But mostly, Doriot instructed his students in the fine art of accomplishment, the value of ethics, and the virtue of work. And he taught them manners. Each new class received the same instructions.

You and I shall be on time and be properly dressed.

This is not a matter of discipline, it's a matter of self-respect. It's a matter of acquiring good business habits and I think you will develop more respect for one another, and after a few months you'll be a little more proud when you come and see your classmates well dressed and on time.

If you cannot come on time, don't come. If you cannot come at all, I don't mind. Call my secretary just the way you would do in business.

As Doriot explained it to his students, dressing properly was simply the way to do business. Otherwise, he held no strong views on the subject, one way or another. For himself, Doriot was always well tailored—at times impeccably so—with a preference for dark suits and blue, button-down shirts. His style was conservative, but there were lapses. He had a penchant for bow ties for example, though he never knowingly allowed his picture to be taken while he was wearing one. And there are those who can remember the General still tramping the labyrinth of Boston's lower Beacon Hill, blanketed—more often than not in a sometimes flapping, seemingly oversized, belted, World War II trench coat, which he himself had helped design while serving with the War Department in World War II.

Those were memorable days, adventuresome times, the war years. There were mountain-climbing expeditions and a trip to the North Pole to test the clothing and equipment in the 26 severest weather conditions, and under actual battlefield stress. And there was that time—he could never forget it—when he defied the Supreme Commander himself, Gen. Dwight D. Eisenhower. "Ignore" was the word Doriot really preferred when recalling his response to Ike's order. But call it what he would, it was defiance nonetheless. Perhaps, even, disobedience. He remembered it well.

U.S. war planners were worried that a too-abrupt reining in of the war-production stampede, which had been let loose to supply the war effort, would be a disastrous jolt to the domestic economy, and might impair its ability to sustain the peace. So the military was alerted to inform the Washington brain trust as soon as battlefield conditions would allow a gradual phasing down of production. That happened first in 1944 when Eisenhower cabled that the worst fighting was over and production should be slowed. But Doriot had his own ideas. He thought the Supreme Commander premature. Events proved him right. When the fighting heated up again after the Battle of the Bulge, the U.S. was ready—thanks to a recently naturalized, recalcitrant, young brigadier general from Boston.

But Doriot had great respect for Eisenhower. One of his prized memorabilia was a 12" x 15" photo of the Supreme Commander in full uniform. It was autographed: "To my friend, Georges Doriot . . . Dwight Eisenhower." Until the end of his life, Doriot prominently displayed that photograph alongside a picture of his beloved Edna, on a bookcase in his study at 12 Lime Street. He deemed it a privilege to have had the opportunity to serve his adopted country in the war years and was perennially grateful. The U.S. was special to him. It rewarded his effort with opportunity, and he seized every chance to repay the favor in whatever way he could. It was, as he often told his students, one of his reasons for teaching.

> So just realize that I am doing it (teaching) because I think that people, knowing that I came to America from France—nobody asked me to come—were nice to me and I stayed here. Therefore, as long as I can do something which is useful to others, I would like to do it.

It was characteristic of Doriot that he would place such a workaday value on his extraordinary talents as an educator—"something which is useful to others." But then someone less competent might not have been as confident. One can't look at something and see how big it is, without knowing how small it is at the same time.

Bernstein was to put it into perspective during his dinner remarks

at Doriot's eightieth-birthday celebration later that day. He chose three
apt quotes from the Bible, comparing Doriot to Moses, as teacher,
philosopher, and man.

> Moses chose capable men out of all Israel and appointed them
> heads over the people. —*Exodus 18:25.*
> Love your neighbor as yourself. —*Leviticus 19:18.*
> Now Moses was a very humble man, more so than any other man on
> earth. —*Numbers 12:3*

And true to the word, Doriot stepped out from behind the lectern;
looked up at his students in Harvard's Burden Hall that bright
September day in 1979, and gazed back in time. The long-awaited
refresher class in Manufacturing began on a humble note.

> From time to time I get slightly sentimental.
> I owe the little I am in this world, I owe it to my wife, to the Business
> School, and to my students . . . to my students who made me.
> Because I did not help you very much.
> I fortunately got, in the second-year course, able men, and all I had
> to do is to give them the opportunity to show to me, and to themselves,
> what it is that they could do. So that's that.
> All I can tell you, or remind you of, are the simple things that we said
> to each other. Because it's the simple things that count in life. The com-
> plicated ones I'm not worried about, you can figure them out.
> I shall give you the beginning of the course and the end, there will be
> nothing in between. But usually, as you know, there was nothing in between.
> I shall remind you of some of the points which I believe that with time
> were important, and as far as I'm concerned, still might be . . .

And once again Burden Hall rang with that awesome admonition,
delivered in a thick French accent and a blunt severity calculated to
arouse the opening-day terrors, in even the boldest of student hearts.

"You and I shall be on time, and properly dressed." It was Doriot's way of getting their attention. How could they have forgotten? The memories came tumbling back.

> I wish you would invite your wives to class, because it will give them a chance to find out what your work is all about, and it might help you team up in life. You can also bring a girl, if you are really interested in her, because it might help you reach your decision.

But there were limits, he reminded them and he was quick to point them out. The warning was implicit; the instruction, clear.

> Do not bring outsiders because I don't like them.
> Don't bring students who are not taking the course; our meeting is a private one.

And as the teacher lectured on, the General took command.

> I shall do all the talking. You listen, think, and make notes of what surprises you, what interests you, what further thinking it suggests to you, and what you think you disagree with.
> Do not ask questions in class. The chances are you will be wasting everybody's time, merely for your own satisfaction. If you have an intelligent question, tell me after class and I shall be glad to take it up at the next class.
> I know modern education calls for participation. I want your mental participation. You see, all of those things are useful in business.
> What I say in class should be accepted by you on a temporary basis until such time as you have thought about it. Then, with your increasing wisdom, you can come to your own temporary conclusions.
> I said don't accept it, but don't reject it, just think about it.

Then Doriot reminded them again of what he considered an essential for a successful life. It was here that Manufacturing turned to the making of men.

I suggest that you start a Manufacturing notebook. It should become
a habit to carry through life. It should become the mirror of your thinking. I repeat, it should become the mirror of your thinking.

He urged his students to think of their notebook as a confidential
companion, and to use it to plan their work, budget their time, record
their thoughts, "measure their mental work," and stimulate their
curiosity and inventiveness. In the voyage of life, one needs a confidential companion, he told them. But the relationship must be nurtured.

"If your book remains empty, start wondering why," he warned
them. It was Doriot's hope Manufacturing would give his students
what he liked to call "a running start" in business and in life. He
reminded them again.

I had a story of a streetcar, an old-fashioned streetcar. And the story
was this: If you stand at rest and try to jump on a moving streetcar, you
break your neck. If you gather speed then jump on the streetcar, you
stay on it, and ride with it
    So that's the attitude I want the students to learn.

It was yesterday all over again: the students were as entranced as
ever; the teacher, in retrospect, even more mesmerizing than ever
before. He had assumed that familiar, dramatic pose of his: standing at
ease in three-quarter profile—his feet slightly apart. Watching them
intently, his probing eyes flitting from face to face. His left hand rested
purposefully in his trouser pocket, like someone used to carrying a
swagger stick under that arm. The right was stretched out to the black-
board behind him, his fingertips encircling the words he had just
scrawled on its surface, giving them emphasis. He was like a field
general explaining a battlefield strategy. There was no question that he
was enjoying himself. And the old wit flashed with the usual cunning
irony. From the *HBS Bulletin*:

As the General taught his refresher course in Burden Hall many a listener must have been whisked back in the mind's eye to an old seat in a Manufacturing class of an earlier day, perhaps in Baker 100 or Aldrich 112. As he spoke, there were frequent interruptions of applause and laughter. As he slipped in each bon mot, many a hearer nodded appreciatively.

Some examples:

Anyone who thinks AT&T should be broken up should be sent to France and told to try to use the telephone system there.

A committee is an invitation to do nothing. Very few committees can perform better than the weakest person. You can't drive a locomotive with a committee.

The time to borrow money is when you don't need it. Your banker is a friend in good times; in bad times he remembers that he is a trustee of somebody else's money.

Nobody sees you as naked as your accountant.

In all, Doriot held his more than 450 "students" enthralled for more than an hour, recalling the field-work assignments, the company studies, the topic reports, the "digging into the future." He reminded them that years before he had suggested an MBA degree should only be valid for fifteen years, but could be extended if the holders could give evidence that they have used their education "effectively and constructively to help others in every way they could." Now he told them:

Without any authority to do so, I thereby extend your temporary degree to life. Let us decide today that you are young again. Let us feel young, class of '79.

Let's set new goals, new ideas, and new visions. Let's not be prisoners of bad habits and non-constructive thoughts. Let us escape from whatever prevents us from being daring, kind, thoughtful, and imaginative. Let us be honest with our families and our nation.

It was vintage Doriot. And he concluded with a final exhortation, remembering Edna, and humility.

> May I end with two thoughts. I hope they are not inappropriate, even though they are sentimental. You have to make many decisions, you are intelligent and experienced. You have great reasoning power. Before you decide on anything, consult your heart, and please realize it should have priority.
>
> And the second is purely personal, but I hope you take it that way and it may mean something.
>
> All my life I loved my Edna as much as I could. As much as I knew how. For forty-eight years we were very close together. Now I say to myself, why did I not love her even more?
>
> Thank you so much for what you're doing for my beloved Edna and for me. You have my most sincere and profound gratitude.
>
> This is a day which I can not possibly forget. To all of you, your wives, your families, I wish good health, happiness at home and at work, and constructive success. Thank you very much.

It was over. Doriot was back in his study at 12 Lime Street. It was close to midnight and he was alone. Dorothy had long since left. And Eda, whom he and Edna had brought from Switzerland more than forty years ago to be their housekeeper retired to her apartment in the basement. But he doubted she was sleeping. More likely, she was straining to hear every sound, in the event he needed her. In that case, he only had to call and she would be there—almost instantly—a thin apparition appearing suddenly at his study door which opened on the back hall. The back hall was Ida's province.

Twelve Lime Street was unusual. It sprawled across a double lot. This was rare for that section of Beacon Hill with its fashionably, squeezed townhouses, the principal architectural features of which consisted of uniform floor stacked on uniform floor in wearisome progression: two, three, sometimes four, stories high.

The Doriot house had two entrances on Lime Street: one on the left end of the property, as you faced the house from the street; the other, seemingly next door, to the right. The first was a nondescript, green, windowless door that would have looked more comfortable set in a garden wall. It was rarely used, except by Ida to avoid company, or when she was receiving deliveries, or putting out the garbage. It opened on a landing that branched off to a staircase leading to the basement, and to a four-step riser, connecting to the back hallway, which ran the length of the building to the kitchen at the rear and which—on the way—accessed to the side entrance to the General's study.

The other entrance was almost equally unpretentious, except that its upper half was crowned with a frame of leaded glass of unknown antiquity. This was the main point of entry. And it opened on a dimly lit, richly polished, wooded vestibule, guarded by two stone lions perched on the head-high sills of the leaded glass windows on either side of the door.

The lions faced inward, glowering protectively over the main foyer beyond, which was three steps higher than the street-level vestibule. Except for a Renaissance-like bureau, under an antique mirror; a pair of wrought-iron sconces, and two pointed-arch, Gothic doors—one leading to a bath on the right and the other to The First Venture Capitalist's study on the left—the foyer was unadorned. But it was quiet. And it had a warm, bronze glow. So the effect on the visitor was one of church-like repose. And straight ahead was the showpiece! The famous Doriot dining room: their sunny, sky-lit dining room! It was his and Edna's favorite. For certain, there was not another room like it in all of Boston.

The house had originally been designed as a blacksmith shop, a two-story structure enclosing an interior center courtyard with living quarters on the second floor. What was now the Doriot dining room was actually the courtyard, roofed over with a skylight. The result was spectacular. Two massive, seven-foot high iron gates—of the kind usually seen decorating the main entrance to city parks, or barring entry to cloistered estates—stand open to allow access to the dining room from the main foyer. To the right, as one enters, is a walk-in stone fireplace with waist-high, black, iron andirons, reminiscent of a Rhineland hunting lodge. The scarred brick wall in which the fireplace is set soars over two stories high—from the terracotta tiled floor, to the aqua-tinted skylight that comprises the entire ceiling of this enchanting room.

The rest of the interior walls are stucco, hung with fine paintings, intricately turned sconces, and rare carvings. Like the brick wall, they reach from the tiled floor to the skylight ceiling—unbroken, except for two interior balconies which overlook the dining area from the massive living room and the main hall on the second floor.

Flowering window boxes and potted plants decorate the balconies. A ficus tree flourishes in one corner, and ivy twines in and out among the grillwork of the imposing iron gates. A Mediterranean garden in the heart of Boston's Beacon Hill.

The birthday party had gone well. After Doriot's refresher class, the celebrants gathered in the Dean's Garden for cocktails. Dinner was at the Kresge Faculty Club. The weather had been perfect. But now it had started to rain. From where Doriot sat at his desk in his study off the foyer, he could hear the soft rattle of the rain on the skylight.

Edna used to love the sound of the rain on the skylight. He could close his eyes and picture the gentle splatter of its drops on the tiles of the dining-room floor. It was almost as though it were raining inside. Or, as Edna once envisioned it with girlish fancy, it was like their own private shower.

He smiled at Edna and she smiled back from the silver frame that held her photograph at the corner of his desk. There were, in all, four photographs of Edna in the small study. But this one was special. He kept it on the desk, because he spent more time there than anywhere else in the house and because she had such a composed, beautiful, loving smile. She must have been very happy when that picture was taken. He could not remember the circumstances now, but it didn't matter. It hurt to think about it. He had never before thought of sadness as physical pain.

The French are right; the liver is the soul of man. Years ago there would have been no question about it. This same feeling he was now experiencing would have been the exquisite pain of love—or jealousy. Now it was the stabbing ache of loss, of loneliness.

Doriot picked up a pen and opened his "Manufacturing notebook." He would take his own advice and write down his thoughts in his notebook. He would write Edna a letter and tell her about the party, and the fact that, in her name, they had raised close to $200,000 for her French Library in Boston. She would be proud. Doriot was glad again that he had remembered to thank them for her. He hoped they did not think him too sentimental, too maudlin—particularly that part where he had spoken of his love for Edna and urged them to follow the dictates of their hearts above all else. But he meant it. He had always felt that way. Probably the most popular class in his course in Manufacturing was the one on "How To Pick A Wife." It was not an affectation. Their marriages, like his own, were important to him. Take the case of Mary B. Few people know of it. It went like this.

Mary B. was one of the better students at Harvard Business School with a consuming desire to take the course in Manufacturing. But she was hesitant. Doriot's reputation intimidated her. Everyone knew he had no patience with students who wasted his time. So she made a point of impressing him early with the fact that her principal goal in life was a career in business, and that marriage, home, and family—if in the picture at all—were secondary considerations at this stage of her life. And she probably believed it.

Recalling the incident to a friend years later, Doriot remembered Mary coming to see him after final exams. She was visibly nervous and he thought it strange, for she was one of his more outgoing and calmer members of the class. After the usual pleasantries, in which she told him how much she had enjoyed the class and how much she had learned, she blurted out that she was going to get married right after graduation. It sounded more like a challenge than an announcement, as Doriot remembered it. And he must have shown some confusion, because before he could react to her news, Mary went on the defensive. She had met her fiancé in Doriot's class, she explained. He was the young man who had been sitting next to her in Manufacturing all year. It was almost as though it was Doriot's fault. And, that being the case, he shouldn't blame her if she happened to give marriage priority over a career in business.

But that was the least thing on Doriot's mind. He was troubled by Mary's impending marriage, all right, but not for the reasons she thought. It was much more serious than that. When Doriot got back to his office, he checked his files. It was as he suspected. Mary had earned a much higher course mark in Manufacturing than her spouse-to-be, and, therefore, was positioned to graduate much nearer the top of the class than he was. And that, the professor knew, would never do. So Doriot—ever mindful of the obstacles to a happy marriage took the marks of both spouses-to-be, averaged them out, and gave each the same grade. It was probably the best wedding present they received, but they never knew they had gotten it. As Doriot so often told his students: Love is everything.

Now alone in his study and listening to the rain patter in the dining room, he could comfort himself with the realization that there was a time when he too had everything. "I was nothing before I met Edna," he once wrote in his notebook, "I was just a Frenchman in America."

He was later to elaborate on this thought in an interview with *The Boston Globe*.

A good wife is a man's biggest blessing, I've done little in this world. What I've achieved was because of her. When an opportunity came,

I took it and worked hard. I didn't want to disappoint her. Many times, though, I was scared stiff.

It is any wonder, therefore, that Doriot should react as he did when an editor for *Fortune Magazine* contacted him in connection with his being named to *Fortune*'s National Business Hall of Fame? It was June 1979 and Edna had been dead almost a year. The editor asked Doriot to what he attributed the successes in his life. It was the "his life" that got him. General Doriot sat down and wrote the editor a poem:

> You wish to write about my life. There was no such thing as "my life." It is still "our life."
> In many ways, perhaps, now, even deeper than ever, It is still "our life."

> The story of my life
> is not a business story.
> It is a love story.
> So deep and profound
> That it cannot be separated.
> No love story ever is.
> God separated us for awhile
> But still, we are together.
> Please do not separate some more
> What must remain as one.
> I am too weak to survive it.
> Please spare me for her sake.
> Do I need to suffer more?
> To be worthy of her?

In the forty-eight years of marriage Doriot wrote hundreds of poems expressing his love for Edna. But he showed that love in whatever way he could—in a thousand little pedestrian, workaday gestures and kindnesses, which he preferred to think of as "fine manners." He recalled, for example, always standing when Edna left a room.

She would say: "Don't stand. I won't turn around." But she always did. I did it as a symbol that I would always look after her. I wish husbands and wives displayed fine manners to each other.

For Edna's part, she reciprocated with "fine manners" of her own. She would scribble little love notes, tender admonitions and gentle reminders on her personal note paper and then stuff them in the pockets of the clothes she packed for him when he was off on one of his many business trips away from home. But, wherever in the world Doriot's business took him, "home" was always with him. Home was important.

I'm French-born. In France the moment it begins to get dark, we close the shutters. It is not a gesture meant to shut out the light. It is to enclose you inside the home. A house is not necessarily a home. A house is a physical place. A home is where your sentiments are. A spiritual haven. It's where you and your wife shut out the disturbances of the outside world and concentrate on each other. A home is where love abides. It is a place of closeness and togetherness. You can see I believe in love.

And Doriot believed in it with the head as well as the heart— although he would deny any intellectuality.

I'm not intellectual. I'm just a non-intellectual who happened to teach at Harvard. Sometimes I try to reason things out, especially life after death and, indeed, if it would be possible to communicate with Edna. All I do is build up furies. It's childish, but I get angry. I realize I am not capable of that kind of super-reasoning. It's all beyond me.

Yet I have a vague notion that we, humans, have senses beyond the traditional ones, senses that we've never been called upon to use. So, finally, I accept a mystery. Life is a mystery. Death is a fact. Life after life is a mystery. So it all comes back to loving doesn't it? Love is what makes everything worthwhile.

"The story of my life is not a business story," Gen. Georges F. Doriot had told the editor of *Fortune Magazine*. "It is a love story."

And so it remains: a love story that began eighty years ago in the modestly austere home of a young foreman in a French bicycle factory, just outside Paris.

APPENDIX A

THE ESSENTIAL DORIOT

ALLAN CONWAY

Conway, a professor of management strategy at the University of Calgary's Haskayne School of Business, outlines the philosophy and principles of Doriot, as they appear in his teachings and practice.

I. Business Strategy and Planning:

1) The noble task is to build constructively in the hope that capital gains will be the reward for intelligent, hard work. One cannot live off the enterprise and vision of preceding generations only (investment, long-term, view requirements).

2) What's more critical is not business administration, but rather business direction.

3) A superior manager sees opportunity when others did not and then did something about it.

4) The importance of vision and mission in directing decisions (the ARD example).

5) Goals as direction.

6) Scientific inquiry and keen insight.

7) The use of "what if" scenarios in planning in the face of uncertainty.

8) The importance of correct information and knowing how to get it (environmental scanning).

9) The importance of being aware of the world around you—analyze environment but know that change will usually come from a new entrant, often from another country. Need then to understand potential competitors as well as current ones.

10) The importance of planning—coordination between different elements and groups involved in planning. The need for an independent process to test and review performance of new products, and redesign; the use of statistical quality control in reviewing and planning.

11) Measures—be industrially, rather than stock-market oriented.

II. Growth or New Venture Strategies:

Also often called management of innovation; this could be separated out into venture capital and new venture development in established companies.

1) Entrepreneurship and spiritual need ◄──► technology and opportunity paradigm.

2) Venture capital is a strategic investment.

3) Characteristics of great entrepreneurs; select managers based on that (motivation and skills).

4) Characteristics of attractive markets; study and select based on those.

5) Understand the customers' needs in spades (intense due diligence required in this aspect), rather than depend on being able to predict the future of technology.

6) Force entrepreneurs or intrapreneurs to go through a lot of hoops to test their resolve as well as to educate them.

7) Sensitivity to the fragile nature of tech start-ups and predictability.

8) Vision for INSEAD, a premier business school in Fontainebleau, France—need to wait to find an appropriate strategy.

9) INSEAD—ideas/sponsors/champions; heart courage and initiative.

10) Uncertainty means you have to believe the person—look for those who do not seek publicity—the quiet manager.

11) Companies must carefully craft a technological strategy—uncertainty requires that you develop and strategize around hunches, not predictions, accompanied with a clear sense of direction.

12) Business is the art of spending money wisely. A time-honored principle immortalized in *Don Quixote*: ". . . my father was reputed to be a rich man, and indeed, he would have been if he had been as skillful in preserving his estate as he was in spending it."

13) People and ideas are our assets; their measurement, our problem.

14) Setting high goals stimulates ability but means you need patience as well to realize their fulfillment.

15) Venture-capital effort and the development of entrepreneurial businesses requires an infrastructure whether in countries or in companies. This infrastructure is not easy to build; the importance of the Massachusetts Institute of Technology in spawning early ARD investments underscores this point—the proper environment for incubating new ventures. In addition, the roles of mentors and champions in the new venture development process are key—confidence and continued faith in people.

III. Keys to Personal Leadership Development:

1) The importance of personal network of acquaintances.

2) Reflection is important, but unfortunately not well practiced.

3) Seek to understand fully and clearly every problem that arises.

4) Operate on policy, not expediency.

5) The idea of alliances and networks. Seeking advice is key, creating a network of advisers is very important.

6) Must be able to foresee a need to gain confidence of those whose advice or resources you desire.

7) Relationship building/reputation; you are judged by the company you keep.

8) Hard work and help from friends.

9) Seek mentorship and coaching.

10) Be curious, scan and analyze the environment, be excited by new things and possibilities.

11) The critical intersection between management, leadership and command; analysis/reflection/action bent; conform and reform.

12) The need to be the one that recognizes opportunity and acts on it.

IV. The Practice of Leadership:

1) The need for harmony between ideals and skills.

2) The leader as a creator of environment—provide the environment that allows individuals to dig up the desire, the willpower, and the pride to do superior work.

3) The leader as teacher, the leader as story teller, the leader as teacher of

how to think about business in the context of everything else that is going on. Successful teachers "act like a teacher and educator" set good example as they understand the idea framework.

4) The leader as teacher—work side by side with employees on special projects. Hands-on training is key, as is mentorship, role modeling (precursor of GE's "workout" process).

5) Leaders choose people and lead in a way that they can do things they did not think possible.

6) Leaders must demonstrate imagination, critical analysis, and be dedicated to attempting to improve the business.

7) Leaders act as role models.

8) The leader sees work as part of a larger mission—make a better society for all (institution builder).

V. Managing Organization Change:

1) We need organizations that can react to change, on a global front.

2) At the individual level, we need personal appetite for change and progressive innovation.

3) Each problem requires new thinking rather than relying on old solutions.

4) We need systems thinking (Taylorism was flawed, so was the HR school). Many human problems come about because of technical errors.

5) Necessary to be strong enough to develop and follow a policy that is not popular.

6) The keys to success: i) understand the structural environmental forces; ii) determine goal-direction is the key, not point; iii) drive effort towards the goal efficiently; 4) determine course of action.

VI. Criticality of Managing the Company/Environment Interfaces:

1) Don't go to Washington for help—accept the results and create the results of your own efforts.

2) Create an environment where the need for government intervention is minimal.

3) Influence the world of legislation to make for good legislation and prevent harmful ones.

4) Businessmen must take an interest in government and in the creation of good government.

5) Technology can cause the building of real businesses that could bring about economic transformation.

6) Business is not about dollars and cents so much as about building for the future.

7) Followers need to follow someone they admire. Companies also need to be admired to attract worker loyalty.

8) Create linkages and goodwill in your environment directly to justify the existence of your business and its need for profits.

VII. Globalization:

1) In going international, don't try to sell what we have but rather what the new customer needs and wants.

2) Practice competitive analysis and measure the threat of foreign players.

VII. Leadership and Values:

1) Sometimes, to be right you must stand alone.

2) Sometimes, it takes great sacrifice to be right.

APPENDIX B

ACCEPTANCES FOR GENERAL DORIOT'S 80TH BIRTHDAY PARTY

On the occasion of Doriot's 80th birthday, a group of former students organized a gathering in Boston. The theme was a 'refresher course' by the general. Invitations were sent to former students. Here is a list of the people who came.

Lee Abramowitz
C. F. Adams
Franklin E. Agnew III
Mr. & Mrs. Vernon R. Alden (Marion)
Louis L. Allen
Mr. William M. Altenburg
Mr. & Mrs. Robert S. Ames
Harlan E. Anderson
Mr. & Mrs. Edward L. Anthony
Robert N. Anthony
Mr. & Mrs. George Appell
David B. Arnold, Jr.
William J. Askin.
Anthony G. Athos
Gayle O. Averyt & Mrs. Averyt
George P. Baker
Mr. & Mrs. Raymond F. Baddour
Professor & Mrs. Marston Balch
Mr. Robert W. Baldridge

Mr. Milton A. Barlow

Mr. & Mrs. Gene K. Beare

Mr. Edward R. Bedrusian

John Belasch

Rod Belden

Janice Bell

Jim Bell

Margery Benson

Richard Arthur Berenson & Spouse

George Berman & Guest (Jugta Hager)

L. Paul Berman

Mr. & Mrs. Sanford C. Bernstein

Mr. & Mrs. Fred F. Berry

Alfred M. Bertocchi

Carl Biehl

Mr. F. Steele Blackall, III

Gerhard D. Bleicken

Halter Blenk

Paul A. Borel

Mr. & Mrs. Allen Boorstein (Jane)

Douglas K. Boyd

Marvin Bower

Robert T. Brady

Mr. & Mrs. Robert R. Bramhall

Mr. John F. Brennan & Kevin Brennan

B. A. Bridgewater, Jr.

William V. Brokaw

J. W. Brougher

V. Ross Brown

Walter I. Brown

Mr. & Mrs. Charles Buchanan

Roger Burke

Mr. & Mrs. Bushman

Mr. & Mrs. Philip Caldwell (Betsy)

Mr. & Mrs. George H. Cannon, Jr.

(Mary Ellen) Frank Chamberlain

Mr. & Mrs. Paul J. Chase

Ms. Susan Chase

Don A. Christensen

Mr. & Mrs. John E. Clark

Patricia Clark

Mr. & Mrs. Lee M. Clegg

Mr. & Mrs. Paul Clinton (Kathy)

Mr. & Mrs. Joseph B. Collinson

Mr. Even Collinsworth, Jr.

Mr. & Mrs. James C. Cook

Leo J. Coveney

Mr. & Mrs. Cliff D. Crosby

Mr. & Mrs. Alexander T. Daignault

Henry B. Dalby

Mr. Richard S. Davis

Ms. Barbara Davis

Mr. & Mrs. Charles S. Diehl

Robert H. T. Dodson

William H. Donaldson

Philip Donham

Mrs. Alfred E. Donovan & daughter (Catharine-Mary)

Arch R. Dooley

Mrs. Elliot du Bois

Mr. & Mrs. T. J. Dermott Dunphy (Joan)

Thomas Dunn

Mr. & Mrs. Chuck Dyer (Karen)

Ms. Helen Drosky

Byron K. Elliott—(for lecture only)

Ted H. Elliott, Jr.

Mr. & Mrs. Long Ellis

Mr. & Mrs. George B. Emeny

Mr. & Mrs. Roger P. Establie (Suzanne)

Mr. & Mrs. Bruce W. Everitt

Mr. & Mrs. Tom F. Faught (Lee)

Mr. & Mrs. Sumner L. Feldberg

J. Brooks Fenno

Ken Fettig

James H. Fisher, Jr.

Mr. Robert M. Foss & Mrs. Foss (Phyllis)

Byron Foster

Mr. & Mrs. Lawrence E. Fouraker (Patricia) & daughter

Mr. Maurice T. Freeman

Mr. & Mrs. Thomas A. Fransioli III

Mrs. Ruth Fritz

E. N. Funkhouser, Jr.

K. Georg Gabriel

Mr. & Mrs. George P. Gardner, Jr.

Mr. & Mrs. Peter Gebhard (Elizabeth)

Mr. & Mrs. James P. Giblin

Mr. & Mrs. James P. Giles, Jr. (Joan)

Mr. & Mrs. Jordan L. Golding (Sandy)

Mr. & Mrs. Arthur L. Goldstein (Vida)

Beverly Graham (Wife of John R. Graham, Sr.)

Mr. & Mrs. Joseph M. Greeley

Mr. Stanley Greenfield

Mr. Vincent L. Gregory, Jr.

Mr. Sandy Hale

Mr. & Mrs. John S. Hamilton

Mr. & Mrs. William R. Haney

Michael B. Harding

Mr. & Mrs. John H. Hardwick

Larry A. Hart

Samuel A. Hartwell

Dr. & Mrs. George N. Hatsopoulos

Mr. Robert R. Hauptfuhrer

Mr. Warren Hayes

Mr. James A. Henderson

Mr. Daniel K. Herrick

Mr. Sigmund Herzstein

Mr. Richard M. Hexter

Mr. & Mrs. William B. Heye, Jr.

Harold B. Higgins

Mr. Richard D. Hill

Mr. & Mrs. Arthur R. Hilsinger, Jr.

Mr. & Mrs. Edward R. Hintz (Helen S.)

Mr. & Mrs. Ralph P. Hoagland III

Mr. & Mrs. Lloyd C. Hoeltzel

Amor Hollingsworth

Mr. Robert Holton

Mr. Gerald J. R. Holtz

Mrs. Mylo Housen

Mr. & Mrs. A. S. Howe, Jr.

Mr. & Mrs. John H. Hughes (Shirley)

Mr. & Mrs. John H. Humphrey

Jerome C. Hunsaker, Jr.

Don Husmann

Mr. & Mrs. Don W. Hutchings

Mr. & Mrs. Kenneth L. Isaacs (son—K.C.A. Isaacs)

Jerry V. Jarrett

Joseph Y. Jeanes, Jr.

William G. Jennings

Franklin P. Johnson, Jr.

Mr. & Mrs. Theodore G. Johnson (Ruth T.)

David J. Jones

Mr. & Mrs. Maurice Kaplan (Charmaine)

Thomas A. Kershaw

James L. Keyes

Mr. Arthur B. King

Harold J. Kingsberg

Mr. Gordon Kingsley

Mr. & Mrs. Michael M. Koerner (Somja M.)

Mr. H. Brewster Kopp

Mr. Louis E. Kovacs

Nicholas La Fauci

Mr. Lee E. Landes

Mr. Herbert H. Lank

Mr. W. J. Ledbetter

Mr. G. R. Lehrer

Mr. Robert Lenzner

Mr. Lawrence Lewin (Ms. Marion Ean—fianceé)

Mr. James T. Lewis

Mr. Lennert Lindberg

Mr. Ralph T. Linsalata & Linda (wife)

Mr. & Mrs. Joseph P. Littlefield

Mr. & Mrs. Howard H. Love

Mr. & Mrs. John E. Lucas

Mr. Robert B. Luick

Mr. & Mrs. John G. Lunn (Twyla Jean)

Mr. & Mrs. Frank Lyman

Sandy A. MacTaggart

Mr. Stephen A. Mandell

Mr. & Mrs. Julius Marcus

Jacques R. Maroni & daughter (Janari)

Mr. & Mrs. John F. Marshall

Chester T. Marvin

Mr. & Mrs. Peter Matthews

Mr. & Mrs. Robert A. McCabe (Dina)

Mr. & Mrs. George E. McCown

Mr. F. Warren McFarlan

Mr. & Mrs. Norman Meyer

Mr. George R. Miller

Mr. & Mrs. Taylor M. Mills

Mr. George Montgomery

Mr. & Mrs. Edgar J. Moor

Mr. & Mrs. James F. Morgan

Mr. & Mrs. Sonny Monosson

Mr. & Mrs. Robert K. Mooney (Barbara C.)

Mr. John R. Moot

Mr. Thomas P. Muchisky

Mr. B. R. Newman

Mr. & Mrs. Warren Nordquist (Carol)

Mr. & Mrs. Elliott D. Novak

Mr. William K. O'Brien

Mr. William P. O'Connor, Jr.

Mrs. Hilda Ochoa

Mr. Kenneth H. Olsen

Stanley C. Olsen

Philip William Orth

Mr. & Mrs. William B. Osgood

Mr. & Mrs. Joseph Ott

Michael Pescatello

Mr. Charles Petschek

Mr. Thomas E. Petry

Mr. James C. Piggot

Mr. & Mrs. Al N. Pilz (Connie)

Mr. & Mrs. David R. Powers (Mary Ann)

Mr. & Mrs. Patrick F. Powers & guest

Mr. Bill Pugh, Jr.

Mr.& Mrs. Dudley Rauch (Cecilia)

Mr. & Mrs. William F. Ray (Helen)

Alexander A. Raydon

Mr. & Mrs. Edward S. Redstone

Mr. Robert A. Reid

Ewing W. Reilley

Albert E. Riley

John E. Riley

Mr. & Mrs. Griff Resor (Pam)

Wyndham Robertson

James D. Robinson III

Mr. & Mrs. James E. Robison

Mr. & Mrs. John G. Roche (Brenda)

Frederick S. Rolandi, Jr.

Mr. & Mrs. Cecil S. Rose

Stuart M. Rose

Mr. & Mrs. Richard Rosenthal (Patricia)

Mr. George Roshkind

Mr. & Mrs. James S. Ross

Miss Dorothy Rowe

Mr. & Mrs. Edward D. Rowley

Mr. & Mrs. David T. Rubin

Henry E. Russell

Mr. & Mrs. Kendall G. Russell (Elaine)

Mr. Walter B. Rust

Mr. Louis C. Ruthenburg

Mr. R. J. Saldich

Mr. Robert Saltonstall, Jr.

Mr. & Mrs. Omar A. Sawadd

Bill H. Sells

Mr. Winfield A. Schuster

Mr. J. A. Shane

Mr. & Mrs. John E. Sheehan

Mr. John J. Shields

Mrs. Marlowe E. Sigal (Elise C.)

Mr. & Mrs. Pierre F. Simon

Mr. Walter Smachlo

Mr. Peter Smith

Mr. & Mrs. Thornton E. Smith

Mr. & Mrs. Verne M. Spangenberg (Susan)

Mr. & Mrs. Holly W. Sphar (Mabel)

Mr. & Mrs. Dennis C. Stanfill

Mr. John C. Staniunas

Mr. Richard A. Stark

Mr. Marshall S. Sterman

Mr. Robert. L. Stix and son (Christopher)

Robert Sykes

E.W. Rich Templeton

Mr. & Mrs. Richard J. Testa (Janet)

Colonel Alan P. Thayer

Mr. & Mrs. William S. Tomkins (Lois V.)

Mr. & Mrs. Marvin S. Traub (Lee) & daughter, Peggy

Mr. Frank L. Tucker

Mr. Richard B. Uhle

Mr. & Mrs. George Ursul

Mr. Richard F. Vancil

Erwin von Allmen

Mr. & Mrs. Wayne Wager (Anne)

Mr. & Mrs. Charles P. Waite

Mr. & Mrs. J. Emerson Wallace

Mr. & Mrs. Leslie H. Warner (Mary)

Mr. & Mrs. James B. Webber (Joan)

Mr. John W. Weber

Mr. David Wechsler

Mr. & Mrs. Sidney J. Weinberg, Jr. (Betty)

Mr. & Mrs. J. Fred Weintz, Jr. (Betty)

Mr. & Mrs. Herbert C. Wells, Jr.

William H. Wendel

Mr. & Mrs. George West (Marion)

George K. Whitney

Mr. & Mrs. H. DeWitt Whittlesey

William P. Wilder

Mr. & Mrs. Robert L. Wiley & son (Mary Ann & Robert L. III)

Mr. & Mrs. James R. Winoker

A. V. Woodworth

INDEX